Students and External Readers	Staff & Research Students
DATE DUE FOR RETURN	**DATE OF ISSUE**

**Any book which you borrow remains your responsibility
until the loan slip is cancelled**

163. Embroidered binding presented to Queen Elizabeth, London, 1583
BODLEIAN

FINE BINDINGS

1500-1700

from Oxford Libraries

Catalogue of an Exhibition

BODLEIAN LIBRARY, OXFORD
1968

The woodcut by Jost Amman on the title-page shows sixteenth-century binders at work. It is taken from Hartman Schopper, Πανοπλια *omnium artium,* printed at Frankfurt-am-Main, 1568.

(From the collection of blocks presented by Bernard Quaritch Ltd.)

Printed in Great Britain by
Alden & Mowbray Ltd
at the Alden Press, Oxford

TABLE OF CONTENTS

PREFACE

The bindings in the Bodleian collections have in the past attracted considerable interest. In 1891 Salt Brassington's *Historic bindings in the Bodleian Library* was published; in the following years, a series of authoritative writings by Strickland Gibson described some of the Library's most significant holdings. A small exhibition of bindings was held in 1937–38. In 1951 appeared the second of the *Bodleian picture books*, under the title *Gold-tooled bookbindings*. This, after an introduction by Mr. I. G. Philip, now Keeper of Printed Books, gave reproductions of twenty-four of the Library's most beautiful bindings, starting with a fifteenth-century Hungarian specimen and ending with a fine French example of the eighteenth century. The bequest of the working collection of Lt.-Col. W. E. Moss in 1953 has greatly assisted the study of the history of bookbinding. The Lyell lectures of M. Jacques Guignard, Conservateur en Chef of the Bibliothèque de l'Arsenal, delivered in 1964, were devoted to French bindings. Much interest was stimulated by them, and was intensified by the exhibition at the British Museum in 1965, organized by Mr. Howard Nixon, of the work of the most celebrated of all patrons of bindings, Jean Grolier. The historical study of bookbinding is now an important part of the professional training of librarians and one with which the Bodleian is specially associated. It has in the last eight years organized several courses on this subject for the Standing Conference of National and University Libraries. This has brought many librarians to Oxford each summer and has drawn particular attention to our collections.

It has now been thought desirable to place on exhibition not only some of the Bodleian's own most treasured bindings, but also examples from other collections in Oxford. The best thanks of the Library are due to those who have agreed to lend for exhibition (and in several cases for reproduction) books and manuscripts from their collections: the governing bodies of twenty-four colleges, the Curators of the Taylor Institution, the Delegates of the University Press, the Trustees of Lord Astor's Books Settlement. A personal word of thanks is also due for their co-operation and helpfulness to the Librarians of the colleges and to the Printer to the University.

The three members of the Library staff who have been most involved in the exhibition are Mr. Giles Barber, Dr. David Rogers, and Mr. Paul Morgan, and to them I should like to express my personal thanks. They have had the advantage of the expert advice of Dr. Neil R. Ker and the continuous, patient, and untiring assistance of Mr. Howard Nixon. To both of them the Library owes a great debt of gratitude, as it does also to those scholars, librarians and collectors who have readily responded to questions and communicated information, often of a recondite character. They are too numerous for all of them to be named but I should like to single out Mr. J. C. T. Oates and Mr. Raphael Esmerian.

The beauty of the bindings exhibited can speak for itself. Bindings are an art-form well worthy of study as such. Their history is also a relatively new bibliographical discipline which can throw important light on the transmission both of the manuscript and the printed word. The preparation of this exhibition has involved its organizers in cataloguing *de novo* many of the bindings listed. It has resulted in the discovery of some hitherto unknown rarities. It is hoped that the catalogue will be of use in future years as a work of reference. Describing as it does bindings executed in a number of countries and now found in Oxford, where many of them found their home more than two hundred years ago, it illustrates the international character of the book trade and of book collecting in the sixteenth and seventeenth centuries.

ROBERT SHACKLETON

INTRODUCTION

This exhibition does not claim to present a history of Western bookbinding between 1500 and 1700 but aims rather at representing the holdings of the Bodleian and the college libraries for this period. Necessarily this has left certain regrettable gaps, in particular by the absence of notable German and Spanish bindings. These gaps are, however, to some extent offset by the number of French and Italian bindings found, an emphasis which, in its turn, perhaps reflects the interests of the collectors and donors through whom these books came to Oxford. It seems unlikely that many of the works exhibited were purchased either by their donors or by libraries for the sake of their bindings; rather, what is exhibited here is in fact largely an aspect of book production accumulated without conscious organization. A few exceptions must of course be made: the embroidered bindings of the 1620s presented to the University and the specially commissioned college benefactors' registers were intended to be fine pieces. Francis Douce and T. R. Buchanan, among Bodley's benefactors, and Sir Thomas Brooke, among Keble's, would, however, appear deliberately to have collected fine bindings; but the interest in bindings as works of art, and their consequent sharp rise in value which makes additions now difficult, are of a comparatively recent date. W. Salt Brassington's *Historic bindings in the Bodleian Library* (1891) appeared in the same year as the Burlington Fine Arts Club exhibition of bookbinding, perhaps the first major public exhibition of this kind. Of recent years the Baltimore exhibition of 1957 and the various catalogues of Major J. R. Abbey's collections have, together with other catalogues and exhibitions, done much to emphasize the artistic importance and interest of fine bindings.

In connection with the preparation of the intercollegiate catalogue of early printed books and that of this exhibition, a rapid survey was made of all post-medieval bindings in the major Oxford libraries and thus, besides those exhibited, it has been possible to refer to other examples in Oxford collections.

Since a number of items come from two or three particular collections, reference to the collector and donor to the present library has, in such cases, been abbreviated. Bodleian benefactors, details concerning whom will generally be found either in W. D. Macray's *Annals of the Bodleian Library* (2nd edition, 1890) or in Sir Edmund Craster's *History of the Bodleian Library 1845–1945* (1952), are normally shown at the end of the provenance entry with the date when their collection reached the Bodleian shown in parentheses. Thus the entries for Francis Douce's (1757–1834) books end: F. Douce (1834), and those for Thomas Rayburn Buchanan's (1846–1911), which were given by his widow in 1941, as: T. R. Buchanan (1941). Similarly those collected by Sir Thomas Brooke (1830–1908) and bequeathed by his younger brother, Charles Edward Brooke, to Keble College in 1911 are shown as: Brooke bequest (1911), and those, mostly acquired by Sir William Clarke (1623–66) when assistant secretary to the Army Council, and left to Worcester College in 1736 by his son George Clarke (1661–1736) as: G. Clarke (1736).

LIST OF PRESENT OWNERS

OTHER THAN THE BODLEIAN LIBRARY

ALL SOULS COLLEGE
   Nos. 4, 7, 14, 16, 17, 23, 37, 43, 78, 101, 103, 106, 120, 147, 178, 179, 206, 207, 208

BALLIOL COLLEGE
   Nos. 40, 59, 72, 80, 125, 160

CHRIST CHURCH
   Nos. 121, 122, 128, 131, 164, 200, 202, 239

CORPUS CHRISTI COLLEGE
   Nos. 22, 74, 108, 124, 169, 215

EXETER COLLEGE
   Nos. 9, 46, 47, 49, 52, 54, 56, 213, 232

JESUS COLLEGE
   No. 137

KEBLE COLLEGE
   Nos. 1, 19, 34, 81, 95, 98, 133, 205, 220, 230, 235

LADY MARGARET HALL
   No. 6

LINCOLN COLLEGE
   No. 221

MAGDALEN COLLEGE
   Nos. 2, 15, 45, 113, 132, 151, 159, 224

MANCHESTER COLLEGE
   No. 117

MERTON COLLEGE
   Nos. 33, 68, 116

NEW COLLEGE
   Nos. 61, 66, 119, 222

ORIEL COLLEGE
   No. 214

OXFORD UNIVERSITY PRESS Printer's library
   No. 223

PEMBROKE COLLEGE
   Nos. 104, 194, 231

QUEEN'S COLLEGE
   Nos. 105, 130, 140, 180, 219

ST. EDMUND HALL
   No. 226

ST. HUGH'S COLLEGE
   No. 136

ST. JOHN'S COLLEGE
   Nos. 39, 65, 109, 110, 126, 139, 142, 161, 167, 191, 204, 217

SOMERVILLE COLLEGE
   No. 87

TAYLOR INSTITUTION
   Nos. 18, 186

TRINITY COLLEGE
   Nos. 62, 67, 228

TRUSTEES OF LORD ASTOR'S BOOKS SETTLE-MENT (*with deposit shelfmarks*)
   Nos. 27(D1), 57(D3), 83(D8), 93(D6), 94(D7), 96(A19), 97(A13), 150(C5), 153(C7), 177(A21), 181(D9), 218(A3), 234(C10), 240(C8)

UNIVERSITY COLLEGE
   Nos. 70, 134, 225, 233

WADHAM COLLEGE
   No. 112

WORCESTER COLLEGE
   Nos. 13, 90, 141, 143, 144, 145, 148, 152, 155, 158, 174, 183, 187, 195, 211

REFERENCES

BALTIMORE   *The history of bookbinding, 525–1950 A.D.*, an exhibition held at the Baltimore Museum of Art. Organized by the Walters Art Gallery. Edited by D. Miner. Baltimore, 1957.

BFAC   Burlington Fine Arts Club, *Exhibition of bookbindings.* London, 1891.

BRASSINGTON   Brassington, W. S., *Historic bindings in the Bodleian Library.* London, 1891.

DE MARINIS, *Fürstenberg*   Marinis, T. de, *Die italienischen Renaissance-Einbände der Bibliothek Fürstenberg.* Hamburg, 1966.

DE MARINIS, *Legatura*   Marinis, T. de, *La legatura artistica in Italia nei secoli XV e XVI.* 3 vols. Florence, 1960.

GIBSON   Gibson, S., *Some notable Bodleian bindings.* Oxford, 1901–04.

GOLDSCHMIDT   Goldschmidt, E. Ph., *Gothic and Renaissance bookbinding.* 2 vols. London, 1928.

HOBSON, *Cambridge*   Hobson, G. D., *Bindings in Cambridge libraries.* Cambridge, 1929.

HOBSON, *English*   Hobson, G. D., *English bindings, 1490–1940, in the library of J. R. Abbey.* London, 1940.

HOBSON, *Fanfares*   Hobson, G. D., *Les reliures à la fanfare.* London, 1935.

HOBSON, *French*   Hobson, A. R. A., *French and Italian collectors and their bindings illustrated from examples in the library of J. R. Abbey.* Oxford, for the Roxburghe Club, 1953.

HOBSON, *Maioli*   Hobson, G. D., *Maioli, Canevari and others.* London, 1926.

MOSS   Moss, W. E., *The English Grolier; the life, lineage and library of Thomas Wotton.* Privately printed, 1941–52.

NIXON, *Broxbourne*   Nixon, H. M., *Broxbourne library* [in the possession of A. Ehrman]. *Styles and designs of bookbindings.* London, 1956.

NIXON, *Grolier*   [Nixon, H. M.], *Bookbindings from the library of Jean Grolier.* London, British Museum, 1965.

NIXON, *Twelve*   Nixon, H. M., *Twelve books in fine bindings from the library of J. W. Hely-Hutchinson.* Oxford, for the Roxburghe Club, 1953.

PHILIP   [Philip, I. G.], *Gold-tooled bookbindings.* (Bodleian picture books, 2.) Oxford, 1951.

SIXTEENTH-CENTURY ITALIAN BINDINGS

For reasons already given in the Introduction, the choice of exhibits in this section, as in certain others, has necessarily been limited; indeed, no exhibition could hope, within the compass of any score of examples that might ideally be available, to do justice to the flowering of fine binding which occurred in Italy during the sixteenth century. Yet a survey of the books here exhibited reveals that although they are confined to four only of the main centres of Italian bookbinding, namely Venice, Milan, Bologna and Rome, they do nevertheless illustrate aspects of cultural history which are at least broadly representative. Even the weighting of examples in favour of Venice (almost half) reflects not unfairly both the dominance of that city as a supplier of books for most of Europe and also its importance as a centre for artistic experiment, creation and transmission. It is fitting, therefore, that the earliest binding exhibited (no. 11) shows a Venetian craftsman trying his hand at the new techniques of gilding and colouring, and applying these to oriental designs, for Venice was the main channel of influence between East and West. How quickly and how surely the techniques were mastered is revealed in the second exhibit in point of time, and the only one from Milan (no. 9). Here, on a manuscript from Petrarch's own library, a binding of consummate quality alike in its workmanship, its taste and design, and even in the materials employed, has been created for that young French collector who (as a later section of this exhibition helps to testify) was soon to become probably the greatest patron of fine bindings in all history.

This interplay of taste between Italy and France is a feature of the century which is further illustrated here in one of the bindings made at Bologna (no. 12) in which a style familiar to the patron from his preceding stay at Paris is probably reflected. The other two Bolognese bindings (nos. 5, 19), though both are on French-printed books, are purely Italian in design. The five examples from Roman binderies go some way to illustrate the importance, in that city, of craftsmen working for great patrons, whether connected directly with the papal court (nos. 17, 21) or among princely and other wealthy families (nos. 6, 14, 16). These Roman bindings have a distinctive flavour of their own, and although these examples do not display the more sumptuous aspects of Roman life, they keep a measure of its dignity through all those changes of fashion which lead from a mid-century simplicity (nos. 6, 14) to a style (no. 21) pointing forward to the next century's baroque.

Great variety of styles is to be expected at Venice, and is in part found among these exhibits. While a binding of about 1530 (no. 20) seems still to handle the new oriental-type ornament in a way which achieves a generally gothic effect, a few years later similar ornaments may be combined to give a wholly Renaissance one (no. 1). Even bindings by the same workshop show complete changes of taste from decade to decade (nos. 8, 10). Two books bound in a richer style were prepared, as might be expected, for special purposes, one for presentation to the Duke of Ferrara (no. 15) and the other perhaps to adorn the publisher's own cabinet (no. 18). Finally, four examples (nos. 2, 4, 7 and 13) illustrate 'trade' work from an important mid-century bindery which takes its title from a patron across the other side of Europe, and demonstrates how far the influence of Venetian wealth and taste could reach.

1 BINDING WITH ARABESQUE CENTRE-PIECE
Venice, c. 1538

All the various motifs here employed can be paralleled in other Venetian bindings, including the cherub heads and the lace-like fringe of small knot tools, and the use of four triangular corner tools to make up the richly effective arabesque centre-piece, but a fourfold overlap of various tools indicates that this book was bound in the Venetian workshop which made three other, and more elaborate, bindings: (1) on a Lyons *Homiliae* printed in the same year, 1538, now at Modena (de Marinis, *Legatura*, II, no. 2044 and plate CCCLXXX) with the same arabesque tools used at the corners, and in the centre the arms of an unidentified owner; this same armorial roundel is on (2) a Dante printed at Venice in 1536 (de Marinis, *Legatura*, II, no. 1367 and plate CCXXXIV, but attributed to Bologna). This Dante has the knot tool and the quadrant corner-pieces of the Keble *Horologion* shown here and shares a number of other tools in common with (3) a manuscript completed at Belluno (a dependency of Venice) in 1559 for Giovanni Cecato da Crepadoni (Baltimore, no. 237; sold at Sotheby's, 10 July 1963, lot 135), which again has the small knot tool and the arabesque corner-pieces of this *Horologion*.

On: ῾Ωρολόγιον, Vinegia, per Stephano da Sabio, a instantia di M. Damian di Santa Maria, 1538.
8°, 155 × 100 × 30 mm. Dark red morocco tooled in gold, re-

backed under the original spine and with the sides inlaid in new boards.

See: G. Fumagalli, *L'Arte della legatura alla corte degli Estensi, a Ferrara e a Modena* (1913), p. 43, no. 184.

Provenance: Brooke bequest (1911).

KEBLE COLLEGE

2   BOUND BY THE 'GRANVELLE BINDERY'   Venice, *c.* 1545

Antoine Perrenot de Granvelle (1517–86), the powerful minister of the Spanish Crown in the Netherlands, who was made a Cardinal in 1561, was also a patron of learning and ranks among the greatest patrons of bookbinding even of that distinguished age. Among the considerable remains of his library preserved at Besançon are one hundred and fifty-seven volumes bound for him in Italy, a large group being sent to him from Venice in 1547 and a further group in 1555 (see M. Piquard, 'Les livres du Cardinal de Granvelle à la Bibliothèque de Besançon. Les reliures italiennes', *Libri*, I (1950–51), pp. 301–23). The Venetian publisher Gabriel Giolito was involved in some way as agent in both transactions, though the bulk of these bindings are not from the workshop which appears to have bound for Giolito himself (cf. nos. 15, 18). Since no fewer than one hundred and thirty-three of the books at Besançon, though falling stylistically into four well-defined groups, are products of a single Venetian workshop, the label of the 'Granvelle bindery' is appropriate for it, though the considerable number of other surviving bindings which share its characteristic types of design and its distinctive array of tools, indicates that it must have operated on an unusually large scale and for many patrons besides the Cardinal. The present binding, with nos. 4, 7 and 13, is the work of this bindery, and together they exemplify two styles which are shared by almost half the group at Besançon. One inconspicuous but very characteristic feature of both is the plain treatment of the spines, which are covered with blind impressions in horizontal bands of a wavy branch enclosing two fir cones.

The three folios here exhibited show variants of design typical of larger books bound in the 'Granvelle bindery'. All three have the same arabesque corner-pieces and single-leaf tool at the outer corners; nos. 2 and 7 share a tool like an uncurling bracken frond, while nos. 4 and 7 have the same border and a pair of branches used

3

with a small pomegranate (these last found again in no. 13). The inner lozenge of no. 4, built up of a variety of short curves, is no less typical of this bindery (cf. no. 13 and Piquard, fig. 3), as are the centre-pieces of all three folios, framed in two concentric circles, nos. 2 and 4 having the device of Fortune (blown about by every wind of chance) which occurs on thirteen of the bindings at Besançon (cf. Piquard, fig. 4) and was, in its different versions, a favourite Renaissance emblem. The particular conformation of the blank shield at the centre of no. 7 is an equally familiar motif of the 'Granvelle bindery' (cf. Piquard, fig. 1). All four volumes originally had four ties each, of coloured silk.

On: THEOPHRASTUS, *De historia plantarum, libri decem* [and other works, being vol. IV of the Aldine edition of Aristotle], (Venetiis, in domo Aldi Manutii, 1497). Hain *1657.
Folio, 307 × 212 × 90 mm. Light brown morocco, tooled in gold and in blind, with remains of four pink silk ties.
Provenance: 'John Goddyr' (Goodyear), who gave many valuable medical and botanical books to Magdalen College about 1664.

MAGDALEN COLLEGE

3 ITALIAN INSCRIBED ARMORIAL BINDING
Venice? c. 1540

The binding on this volume, though the manuscript it contains was written for a religious house in Florence, does not appear to be Florentine in style. Its affinities seem rather to be with Venice. The centre of the oval cartouche on each cover has been ruled in blind into squares, and these have been painted (cf. nos. 15, 16) on the lower cover to give a coat of arms *checky argent and azure*, unfortunately the arms of more than one Italian family. The clue to the original owner of this binding is doubtless contained in the inscriptions tooled in gold round the centre panel of each cover, FVLCITE ME FLORIBVS, STIPATE/ME MALIS, QVIA./AMORE LANGVEO. [Song of Songs 2, 5].S. ЛF. ND ·∴/(upper cover), and SICVT LILIVM SPINAS./SIC AMICA MEA./ INTER FILIAS. [*ibid.*, 2, 2]. S. ЛF. ND (lower cover), where the final letters after each quotation may contain some abbreviation of the name of the owner, possibly a nun.

On: Portable psalter and hours, Italian manuscript of the late fifteenth century written on vellum for a Bridgettine house,

4

which the saints mentioned in the litany show to have been San Salvatore (Il Paradiso), outside Florence.

170 × 120 × 63 mm. Dark red morocco, gilt tooled; rebacked under the original spine. One clasp (from the upper to the lower cover) remains.

See: Van Dijk, Handlist of the Latin Liturgical Manuscripts in the Bodleian Library (typescript), II, fol. 37; Bodleian Library, *Summary Catalogue of Western Manuscripts*, IV, p. 338, no. 19249.

Provenance: San Salvatore outside Florence; 'Abate Calanacci' (sixteenth century); Matteo Luigi Canonici (1727–1805), a large part of whose manuscripts was bought by the Bodleian in 1817.

BODLEIAN (MS. Canon. Liturg. 49)

4 BOUND BY THE 'GRANVELLE BINDERY' Venice, *c.* 1545

See no. 2. This and no. 7 are companion pieces.

On: SIMPLICIUS of Cilicia, Ὑπόμνημα εἰς τὰς δέκα κατηγορίας τοῦ Ἀριστοτέλους, (Venice, Zacharias Callierges for Nicolaus Blastus, 1499). Hain *14757.

Folio, 325 × 228 × 40 mm. Red morocco, tooled in gold and in blind. There were originally four purple silk ties.

Provenance: Given to All Souls College by Sir John Mason (1503–66), the statesman and one-time Chancellor of the University. Mason probably acquired this and no. 7 during his service abroad as a diplomat.

ALL SOULS COLLEGE

5 BINDINGS WITH DEVICE Bologna, *c.* 1540

There is evidence to connect bindings showing the basic elements of the present design—often having at their centre an elegant ogival frame of gilt branches enclosing the book's title, with sometimes a device (Cupid, Fortune, &c., the whole frequently set in blind-tooled borders—with Bologna. Besides these two volumes, which belong to a set of the pocket edition of the Latin Bible published in eight or nine parts by Simon de Colines at Paris between 1522 and 1544, a number of other books printed outside Italy are similarly bound, and this is readily understandable in a celebrated university city where bookshops and binderies served an academic public drawn from all over Europe (see, for example, no. 12).

The band of repeated ornaments (not, apparently, a roll) used in blind round the edges of these two volumes seems to be that used on a Bolognese manuscript dated 1526 (de Marinis, *Legatura*, II, no. 1289 and plate ccxxiii); the same tool is on a Cicero of 1521 (*ibid.*, no. 1308 and plate ccxxv); and on an Aristophanes printed at Basle in 1532 (Gumuchian catal. XII, no. 62 and plate xxix) where the fleur-de-lys is the same. An almost identical binding from the same workshop was made for the Umbrian lawyer Flavius Florianus about 1531 on two works of Haymo printed at Cologne (Breslauer catal. 98, no. 81 and plate II). For a later use of the same border and a similar centre-piece, see no. 19.

On: (1) *Pentateuchus Moysi*, Parisiis, in officina Simonis Colinaei, 1532.
(2) *Liber Psalmorum* (bound with) *Libri Salomonis, ibid.*, 1538, 1537.
16°, 118 × 77 × 30 mm. Dark brown morocco, tooled in gold and blind. Traces of green cloth ties across the upper and lower edges as well as two across the fore-edges.
Provenance: Sir William Fettes Douglas (1822–91), sale by Dowell, Edinburgh, 7 Dec. 1891, lot 71; T. R. Buchanan (1941).

PLATE I   BODLEIAN (Buchanan g.19, 20)

6   BOUND BY THE FARNESE BINDERY   Rome, *c.* 1545

A pleasing example of the effect which early Italian binders could achieve by the use of only a few simple tools. The centre-piece, made by two impressions of a floriated tool, is of a design which recurs at this period in several minutely different versions; a closely similar one is found on a binding presumably made at Rome since it bears the device of the del Monte family whose most illustrious member ruled as Pope Julius III from 1550 to 1555 (see de Marinis, *Fürstenberg*, pp. 58–9). The three smaller tools used here are found on bindings made by the Roman workshop which produced the famous group of bindings having at their centre the Apollo and Pegasus medallion. These were made for a patron long described as Demetrio Canevari, but now considered to be a member (not yet identified) of the Farnese family.

6

On: PINDAR, *Olympia Pythia* [&c.], (Venetiis, in aedib. Aldi, et Andreae Asulani Soceri, 1513).

8°, 157 × 105 × 30 mm. Dark red morocco, tooled in gold and in blind. Traces of two cloth ties.

See: Hobson, *French,* p. 127; de Marinis, *Legatura,* I, pp. 62–8, nos. 686–813 and plates CXXIII–CXXXI; III, p. 97, nos. 2992 bis–2995 and plate G4.

Provenance: Rinaldo Buti (early nineteenth century); sale of the library of Giovanni Marchetti of Turin, Sotheby's, 27 Nov. 1876, lot 1448; Charles George Milnes Gaskell; bequeathed to Lady Margaret Hall in 1931 by Edward Hugh Norris Wilde.

LADY MARGARET HALL

7 BOUND BY THE 'GRANVELLE BINDERY'   Venice, *c.* 1545

See no. 2. A companion binding to no. 4.

On: THEMISTIUS, *Omnia . . . opera* [&c., in Greek], (Venetiis, in aedibus haeredum Aldi Manutii, & Andreae Asulani, 1534).

Folio, 318 × 212 × 35 mm. Red morocco, tooled in gold and in blind; there were originally four pink silk ties.

Provenance: Given to All Souls College by Sir John Mason, as no. 4.

ALL SOULS COLLEGE

8 DUCALE, OFFICIALLY BOUND FOR MICHAEL BONO
Venice, 1564

Among the acquisitions of Archbishop Laud presented by him to the Bodleian during the year 1635 is a group of five manuscript commissions all addressed to the same Michael Bono during his career as an official of the Venetian state and ranging in date from 1552 to 1578. Large numbers of these Venetian commissions survive and since they often have tooled on the upper cover the recipient's name and on the lower cover the date of issue (details which are anyhow known also from the contents), they afford the student of bookbinding history a rich series of dated examples of official Venetian binding, mostly emanating from a small number of workshops regularly patronized by the State.

The earliest of the Bono group, that of 1552 (MS. Laud Misc. 710; de Marinis, *Legatura,* I, no. 1867) is bound in a plain style typical of the 1540s and early 1550s; almost identical bindings are on two similar commissions, also in the Bodleian, dated 1548 (MS. Buchanan d.5) and 1550 (MS. Laud Misc. 712). By the 1560s a more elaborate treatment began to come into vogue, and the present example of 1564, which is by the hand that bound another ducale, dated 1561, illustrated by de Marinis (*Legatura*, II, no. 1891 and plate CCCLII) marks the change. Surprisingly, the second Bono example exhibited here (no. 10) represents a total change of style by 1572, yet individual tools, the slapdash handiwork, and the overall confusion of the design, betray that it is from the same workshop as this 1564 example. The introduction of 'azured' (i.e. hatched) tools possibly indicates French influence, and certainly points forward to a style which was to become typical of Italian bindings of the last quarter of the sixteenth century.

On: Ducale, manuscript on vellum containing commission and instructions in Latin and Italian, addressed to Michael Bono as Podestà of Friuli, and dated 5 May 1564.
233 × 170 × 40 mm. Crimson morocco, tooled in gold. Low on the spines of this and no. 10 are two slits from which there hung originally a small cord with the official seal.

See: For this and no. 10, H. O. Coxe, *Catalogi codicum manuscriptorum Bibliothecae Bodleianae pars secunda*, p. 507; de Marinis, *Legatura*, II, nos. 1783–1917 and plates CCCXL–CCCLV; III, nos. 3145, 3147–50.

Provenance: Archbishop Laud (1635).

BODLEIAN (MS. Laud Misc. 711)

9 PLAQUETTE BINDING FOR JEAN GROLIER
Milan, *c.* 1509–15

On the death of his father in 1509, Jean Grolier (1479?–1565) succeeded him as treasurer of the Duchy of Milan, which had been occupied by the French since 1499. To the beginning years of his service at Milan belongs the earliest group of fine bindings which have survived from the library of the great French bibliophile. Twenty-seven of these bindings are known which were decorated for Grolier with 'plaquettes'—decorative medallions cast from moulds—of which the present example, covering a manuscript from the library of Petrarch, is one. What may be Grolier's arms are painted on the fore-edge, and on the lower half of the last leaf of text, now cut away, was perhaps his own autograph inscription. Both these methods of marking his ownership are found in Grolier's 1499 Suidas (Nixon, *Grolier*, 4, plate IV) now at Trinity College, Cambridge, a closely similar binding on which the same two plaquettes are used.

On: C. SUETONIUS TRANQUILLUS, De vitis duodecim Caesarum, Italian manuscript of the fourteenth century on vellum, probably written for Petrarch, and with his autograph annotations.
348 × 245 × 24 mm. Brown morocco with gilt and blind tooling.
See: Nixon, *Grolier*, 3, plate III; de Marinis, *Legatura*, III, no. 2660 and plate A5.
Provenance: Francesco Petrarcha; Francesco il Vecchio da Carrara, signore di Padova; Visconti Library, Pavia; Jean Grolier; Henry Drury sale, 19 Feb. 1827, lot 4263; entered Exeter College Library between 1868 and 1895.

EXETER COLLEGE (MS. CLXXXVI)

10 DUCALE OFFICIALLY BOUND FOR MICHAEL BONO
See no. 8.

Venice, 1572

On: Ducale, manuscript on vellum containing commission and instructions in Latin and Italian, addressed to Michael Bono as Podestà of Bergamo, and dated 17 Mar. 1572.
233 × 170 × 35 mm. Crimson morocco, gold tooled. The spine preserves the string from which hung the seal.
Provenance: Archbishop Laud (1635).

PLATE II   BODLEIAN (MS. Laud Misc. 713)

11 BOUND FOR NICOLAO FRANCO, BISHOP OF TREVISO
Venice, *c.* 1490

This binding must have been commissioned before the death of its first owner, who was Bishop of Treviso from 1486 to 1499. It belongs to a group of early gilt Venetian bindings which show direct borrowings from oriental, in particular Persian, models. From the East, to which Venice by her trading position was uniquely linked, came not only the style of decoration but also the use of gilding and of colour. The oriental motifs at the centre of this design are freely rendered,

9

chiefly by means of a set of curves which are sometimes gilded, sometimes filled in with black, relieved by touches of paint applied to indentations in the leather, presumably to escape wear from rubbing. At the four corners of each cover are the initials NFET, standing for Nicolaus Francus Episcopus Tarvisiensis, and his arms, made up from small tools, are worked into the centre of the design.

On: St. JEROME, Martyrologium, manuscript written by Pierantonio Sallando, probably in Padua 1486–89, on vellum, with the arms of Franco painted at the foot of the first leaf.
230 × 145 × 30 mm. Brown morocco over wooden boards, rebacked in the eighteenth century.

See: Bodleian Library, *Summary Catalogue of Western Manuscripts*, IV, p. 377, no. 19396; de Marinis, *Legatura*, II, pp. 54, 77 (no. 1633), 78 (no. 1643 bis, another entry for the same binding), and plate C25.

Provenance: Nicolao Franco; Matteo Luigi Canonici (as no. 3).

PLATE III   BODLEIAN (MS. Canon. Liturg. 301)

12 BOUND FOR NICOLAUS VON EBELEBEN
Bologna, 25 July 1543

Nicolaus von Ebeleben and Damianus Pflug, both the sons of Saxon noblemen, were friends and fellow-students at the university, first at Leipzig and later at Paris (1541–42) and Bologna, where Ebeleben remained from 1543 to 1548. During their stay abroad each commissioned fine bindings, which bear his name and also the date and place of binding, thus affording unusually exact evidence for use by historians of bookbinding. After his return home Ebeleben continued to commission bindings for his library which, at his death in 1579, numbered four hundred volumes.

With the exception of an additional rosette, four times repeated, the whole design of this binding is identical with that on a copy of vol. II of the same Aldine edition of Cicero's *Orationes* bound at Bologna in February of the same year for Damianus Pflug (later owned and described by E. Ph. Goldschmidt), which suggests that each friend bought a set of this three-volume Aldine edition and had it bound in the same year by the same workshop, which is that which produced most of their surviving Bolognese bindings. The general design is also that of a Quintilian bound for Ebeleben at Bologna in June of that year (no. 3 in Goldschmidt's census, afterwards lot 1186

in the sale of the library of Lt.-Col. W. E. Moss, Sotheby's, 2 Mar.
1937). A very similar design and identical tools are also found on
a book bound for Ranuccio Farnese (1530–65) between 1543 and
1545 (see de Marinis, 'Di alcune legature fatte per Paolo III,
Alessandro e Ranuccio Farnese', in *Scritti vari dedicati a Mario
Armanni* (1938), p. 43 and plate 18, and his *Legatura*, II, no. 1358).

On: M. T. Cicero, *Orationum volumen primum*, Venetiis, apud Aldi
   filios, 1540.
   8°, 163 × 106 × 30 mm. Light red morocco, gold tooled.
See: Goldschmidt, I, pp. 271–5 (no. 5 of his census), II, plates
   LXXII–LXXIII; Philip, p. 4 and plate 4; Hobson, *French*,
   p. 131, no. 62; Nixon, *Broxbourne*, pp. 52–3, no. 24; Baltimore,
   p. 98, no. 220; de Marinis, *Legatura*, II, p. 25, no. 1378.
Provenance: Nicolaus von Ebeleben; Dr. Joannes Christophorus Seiff
   of Frankfurt-am-Main, 1743; apparently entered the Bodleian
   before 1795.

BODLEIAN (Auct. 2 R 4.68)

13   A SMALL VOLUME FROM THE 'GRANVELLE BINDERY'
Venice, *c.* 1541

Though so obviously differing in design from the three folios (nos. 2,
4 and 7) bound by the same bindery (with which it nevertheless
shares several tools in common and identical blind-tooling on the
spine) this binding is no less typical of the Granvelle bindery's
treatment of books of smaller format. Indeed the design on its octavos
is repeated even more closely than those on larger volumes. Among
more than a dozen examples studied, two of which were bound for
Granvelle himself (Piquard, fig. 2 and E. Ph. Goldschmidt, catal. 8
(1926), item 227) the pattern of the inner lozenge built up of small
curves (cf. no. 4) varies only in detail; the centre panel is frequently
formed, as here, of two ogival arches flanked by large pomegranate
tools and often frames the name of the author and the title of the
book or the owner's name, while the same two arabesque corner-
pieces, which are undoubtedly a pair despite a slight but marked
asymmetry, are regularly found. Closest of all to the present binding
are (1) an Aldine Terence of 1541 in brown morocco (sold at
Sotheby's, 19 Mar. 1896, lot 824) still preserving its green silk ties,
and (2) the only recorded book from Thomas Maioli's library in an
Italian binding, no. LIII in Hobson's list and thought by him to have

been bought already bound, the collector having merely added his name on the lower cover after purchase.

On: VEGETIUS, *De l'arte militare nela commune lingua novamente tradotto per Messer Tizzone di posi,* In Venetia, 1540 (colophon: per Comin da Trino, 1541).
8°, 160 × 103 × 20 mm. Brown morocco, tooled in gold and in blind, with remains of two green silk ties.

See: M. Piquard, 'Les livres du Cardinal de Granvelle à la Bibliothèque de Besançon. Les reliures italiennes', *Libri,* I (1950–51), pp. 301–23; Hobson, *Maioli,* pp. 46, 92 and plate 53 (this volume was afterwards lot 293 in the Mortimer Schiff sale, Sotheby's, 23 Mar. 1938).

Provenance: Daniel Vere (seventeenth century); G. Clarke (1736).

WORCESTER COLLEGE

14 BOUND BY THE 'FARNESE BINDERY' FOR I. RUIZI
Rome, *c.* 1552

More than twenty bindings, on books dated between 1516 and 1569, are now recorded bearing the present arms, which belonged to the Ruizi family, of Spanish origin but domiciled in Rome. The initials of a member of this family, I.R. (not yet identified), flank the central cartouche in nearly all these bindings. This collector tended to favour plain designs for his smaller-sized books, such as the present, but some of his folios are very richly ornamented; all are products of the 'Farnese bindery', which 'seems to have started work about 1545 and from 1550 till about 1572 enjoyed a monopoly of Vatican patronage' (Hobson, *French,* p. xxxv).

A point of interest is the early use of titling on the spine, which in this and the Goldschmidt and Fürstenberg examples, and also on four Ruizi bindings in the Bodleian (8° I 277–279 BS.; Vet. F1 f. 97), is part of the original tooling; under the front pastedown of this All Souls volume is written the actual lettering 'Isto: di Vinetia' which the finisher was to follow.

On: P. BEMBO, *Della historia Vinitiana . . . volgarmente scritta libri xii,* In Vinegia, (Gualtero Scotto), 1552.
4°, 220 × 159 × 30 mm. Brown morocco, gilt tooled.

See: Hobson, *Maioli,* p. 126, nos. 16–19; Goldschmidt, I, p. 289; II, plate LXXXIII; Hobson, *French,* p. 143, no. 69; de Marinis,

Legatura, I, p. 77, nos. 944–9 and plates CLVIII–CLIX; III, p. 99, no. 3010 bis; de Marinis, *Fürstenberg*, pp. 66–67.

Provenance: I. Ruizi; De Pigis (seventeenth century); in All Souls Library by the eighteenth century.

ALL SOULS COLLEGE

15 BOUND FOR PRESENTATION TO ALFONSO D'ESTE
Venice, 1559

For occasions when no metal stamp of the owner's or patron's arms was available, the binder often used paint instead (cf. no. 16), as on this book which is the presentation copy sent by the author to Alfonso II d'Este (1535–97), Duke of Ferrara, to whom the book is dedicated. The upper cover bears the Duke's arms painted and gilded and the tooled inscription 'TV DECVS OMNE TVIS', the lower cover the dedication lettered 'ALL' ILLVSTRISS. ET ECCELLENTISS. SIG. IL. SIG. DON ALFONSO DA ESTE .V. DVCA DI FERRARA'. Some of the details of this typically Venetian binding are to be found on a Venetian edition of Ariosto dated 1556 (de Marinis, *Legatura*, II, no. 2270 and plate C52) which includes a variant of the oval phoenix device of Gabriel Giolito, the Venetian publisher, and is therefore connected with him either through binding or ownership (or both) though it is not by the same hand as no. 18. Again, the present version of a large pomegranate tool is extensively featured on a volume (de Marinis, *Legatura*, II, no. 2469 and plate CCCCVII—the date should be 1559 not 1558) printed by Giolito in this same year 1559 and bound for presentation to Cardinal de Granvelle, though not belonging to the most extensive group of his bindings (cf. nos. 2, 4, 7 and 13). These two pieces of evidence seem to point to a bindery which at least worked for Giolito, as the source of the present binding.

On: G. LANTERI, *Duo libri . . . del modo di fare le fortificationi*, In Vinegia, appresso Bolognino Zaltieri, (1559).

4°, 230 × 164 × 20 mm. Olive green morocco tooled in gold and blind, with painted arms; traces of four ties.

See: BFAC, plate XXV.

Provenance: Alfonso II, Duke of Ferrara; acquired in 1587 by Sir Arthur Throckmorton, M.P. (1557–1626) and bequeathed by him to Magdalen College in 1626.

PLATE IV MAGDALEN COLLEGE

13

A manuscript note at the foot of the title-page records that this copy of the *Pontificale* was presented in 1587 by Francesco Maria Piccolomini, Bishop of Montalcino and Pienza, for the use of the chapel built by himself 'outside his little native town' (extra oppidulum paternum). Piccolomini, who became bishop of Montalcino in 1554, and ruled the united sees of Pienza and Montalcino until his death in 1599, was clearly a relative of the great Sienese family, but the use of the diminutive 'oppidulum' suggests his reference is to Pienza, the birthplace of the Piccolomini Pope Pius II, who had erected his native village of Corsignano into a miniature cathedral city by a series of magnificent buildings and renamed it after himself.

Written inside the back cover is a statement that on 3 October 1587 the bishop gave and blessed various episcopal vestments for use in his chapel, and at the foot of the same cover is the note: 'Venne di Roma, a li xx di luglio, 1587. Costo legato scudi cinque, et julij otto', showing that the volume was bought ready-bound from Rome. The title, the donor's name and his arms were added in paint (cf. no. 15) probably after the book reached Pienza.

On: *Pontificale Romanum*, Venetiis, apud Juntas, 1582.
   Folio, 372 × 264 × 50 mm. Light brown morocco, gold tooled and painted. Traces of two blue silk ties.
Provenance: Francesco Maria Piccolomini; Chapel of St. Francis outside Pienza (?); in All Souls Library by the early nineteenth century.

ALL SOULS COLLEGE

17 BINDING WITH THE ARMS OF POPE SIXTUS V
Rome, *c.* 1590

There can be no doubt that this binding was made in, or very soon after, 1590, the date of this book's publication, though not necessarily in the lifetime of Pope Sixtus V, who died on 27 August of that year. The reason is that despite the publicity which surrounded this, the first official text of the Vulgate to be issued since the Council of Trent, as an edition it received very adverse judgement, and was withdrawn within two years by order of Pope Clement VIII in favour of the 'Clementine' Vulgate. After 1592, therefore, copies would no longer be wanted for any but historical and critical interest.

The presence of the Pope's arms does not imply that this was a personal copy; for the Pope who personally sponsored this Sixtine edition only the most sumptuous possible binding would be appropriate, whereas this is no more than a good representative Roman binding in the monumental style of the last decade of the sixteenth century. It is quite likely that this is one of a number of large-paper copies which would have been got ready for presentation but possibly never so used because of the swift eclipse which overtook this edition.

On: *Biblia sacra Vulgatae editionis,* Romae, ex Typographia Apostolica Vaticana, 1590.
Folio, large paper copy, 418 × 300 × 80 mm. Dark red morocco tooled in gold and with fillets in blind, the corners repaired and the spine rebacked in the eighteenth century. Traces of two leather ties.

See: T. J. Pettigrew, *Bibliotheca Sussexiana* (1827), I, pt. II, pp. 447–66.

Provenance: Sale of the library of Sir Mark Masterman Sykes, Evans, 11 May 1824, lot 610, to Pettigrew for the Duke of Sussex; sale of the library of Augustus Frederick, Duke of Sussex, Evans, 1 July 1844, lot 1170.

ALL SOULS COLLEGE

18   BOUND FOR (AND BY?) GABRIEL GIOLITO
Venice, 1555

This hitherto undescribed binding makes a new addition to a small group of books already known, all bearing on their covers this version of an oval device of a phoenix, which most closely resembles the printer's mark of Gabriel Giolito de' Ferrari, one of the principal Venetian publishers of his time. The possibility (first suggested by A. N. L. Munby in *The Book Collector,* I (1952), p. 129) that such volumes were not just 'trade bindings' from the workshop of the publisher Giolito, but were bound for his own personal library, rested in part on the fact that none of the five other works so bound was printed by Giolito himself. But the present example does not weaken this argument, for if he possessed a private collection it would be inconceivable that it should not contain books from his own press, such as this. The other books of the group were all printed between 1544 and 1555 and those of earlier date are generally of very sober design. The present binding uses much more freely the tools found on those earlier examples, and adds a further pair of tools and an arabesque border, achieving thereby a much richer decorative effect, worthy of a distinguished printer who published many editions of this great poem.

On: L. ARIOSTO, *Orlando Furioso*, Vinegia, Gabriel Giolito de' Ferrari et Fratelli, 1555.

4°, 236 × 164 × 40 mm. Red morocco, gold tooled. Spine redecorated in the nineteenth century. Traces of four green cloth ties.

See: Nixon, *Broxbourne*, p. 68, no. 32; de Marinis, *Legatura*, I, nos. 910–13 and plate CLIII (the phoenix device in II, no. 2270 and plate C52 is closely similar but another version); de Marinis, *Fürstenberg*, p. 163 (another volume from Lord Vernon's set of Cicero in eight volumes, offered in Martin Breslauer's catal. 67, item 28. The Broxbourne example is from the same set).

Provenance: William Horatio Crawford sale, 12 Mar. 1891, lot 164.

TAYLOR INSTITUTION

19 BINDING WITH CRUCIFIXION STAMP Bologna, *c.* 1556

Although this binding might at first sight appear to be Venetian, there are several stylistic indications pointing to Bologna as its true source. The border here is made up of the same tool used in blind on no. 5, and the treatment of the centre-piece is very reminiscent of that shown on a 1543 Bessarion sold at Sotheby's, 19 Dec. 1960, lot 15, which was undoubtedly bound at Bologna.

On: Breviarium Romanum, Lugduni, apud Theobaldum Paganum, 1556. Weale-Bohatta, *Bibliographie der Breviere*, no. 216, = no. 215.

4°, 289 × 210 × 49 mm. Dark red morocco, tooled in gold. Metal and leather clasp across the upper and lower edges as well as two across the fore-edges (see no. 5), the leather gilt-tooled with the border tool. Elaborate knot-work gauffering on the gilt edges.

Provenance: Dr. Claudius Maria Guidottus (seventeenth century); Brooke bequest (1911).

KEBLE COLLEGE

This first edition of the *Introduction* of Simplicius also incorporates the first printing of the Greek text, albeit incomplete, of the *Enchiridion* of the moral philosophy of Epictetus compiled by the latter's pupil Arrian. Brunet (5th ed., vol. II, col. 1011) makes the positive assertion that when Gregorius Haloander, the distinguished jurist born at Zwickau in 1501, published his edition of the *Enchiridion* at Nuremberg in 1529, he worked from a manuscript and did not know the preceding edition, which had appeared at Venice a year earlier. This book, which is Haloander's own copy of the Venice edition, shows that Brunet's assertion is unlikely to be wholly true. Haloander, after two years' study in Italy, had returned to Germany in 1527 to edit the text of Justinian, and was living at Nuremberg when this Venice edition was published. It seems more likely that on its publication in 1528 one of his humanist friends had it bound and sent to him at Nuremberg, than that he bought it himself after his return to Italy in 1531 (the year of his death at Venice), two years after his own edition of the *Enchiridion* had appeared in Germany. But by whichever means this copy became Haloander's, the binding, which is in very typical Venetian style, must date between the book's publication in July 1528 and his own death in Sept. 1531. The upper cover bears the title in Greek: ΣΥΜΠΛΙΚΙΟΣ ΕΙΣ ΕΠΙΚΤΗΤΟΝ, and the lower cover, also in Greek, the owner's name: ΓΡΗΓΟΡΙΟΣ ΑΛΟ-ΑΝΔΡΟΣ. The same border roll was used on a 1527 Priscian now in the Fürstenberg collection (de Marinis, *Fürstenberg*, pp. 134–5).

On: SIMPLICIUS of Cilicia: Ἐξήγησις εἰς τοῦ Ἐπικτήτου Ἐγχειρίδιον, (Venetiis, per Ioan. Antonium & Fratres de Sabio, 1528).
4°, 207 × 148 × 20 mm. Brown morocco, richly tooled in blind, the title and owner's name in central panels in gold.
Provenance: Gregorius Haloander; in the Bodleian by 1605.

BODLEIAN (Auct. K 4.16)

21 BOUND BY A PAPAL COURT BINDERY   Rome, *c.* 1595

Details of the tooling indicate that this binding should be attributed to a workshop which produced three bindings which bear the arms of a prelate of the Roman family of Torres, possibly Lodovico de Torres before he was made a Cardinal in 1606 and Librarian of the Holy Roman Church in 1607. The first of these bindings is on a large paper copy of the Clementine Vulgate (Rome, Vatican Press, 1592), auctioned at Sotheby's on 21 Feb. 1927, lot 643. This has the 'Tudor rose', and also an azured leaf tool, in common with the present binding. The second and third are in the Fürstenberg collection (de Marinis, *Fürstenberg*, pp. 82–83 and 86–87), one on a Psalter (Rome, Vatican Press, 1593) issued for use in St. Peter's Basilica, the other on a Cologne book printed in 1602, the latter having the same azured leaf tool. The present volume being also issued from a Vatican press, the group together suggests a bindery working for members of the papal court. For two later bindings from the same workshop see nos. 173 and 179.

On: CLEMENT VIII, Pope, *Brevis orthodoxae fidei professio, quae . . . ab Orientalibus facienda proponitur . . . Iussu . . . Clementis Papae VIII* [in Arabic and Latin], Excussum Romae, in Typographia Medicea, 1595.
    4°, 222 × 147 × 8 mm. Light red morocco, tooled in gilt, with traces of four silk ties.
Provenance: John Selden (1659).

BODLEIAN (4° P 19 Th. Seld.)

FRENCH BINDINGS OF THE EARLY AND MIDDLE SIXTEENTH CENTURY

Printing was first established in Paris around 1470 and major booksellers appeared there as established traders some twenty years later. The early bindings of this period were mostly blind-stamped and fine books were generally bound in velvet until morocco came in around 1540 (see no. 27). The first major bindery producing gold-tooled bindings worked at Blois for Louis XII between 1503 and 1516, but though some of the tools used were of Italian inspiration the general designs were closer to the earlier blind-stamped work. No example of the work of this bindery is known in Oxford.

Successive monarchs from Louis XII (1498–1515) and François I (1515–47) patronized the trade and appointed royal binders, but a growing class of private collectors also exercised much influence and none perhaps more so than Jean Grolier (1479?–1565), Treasurer of France and the greatest of all French bibliophiles (see nos. 23, 24, 31). His library, which he began collecting in Italy during the campaigns there (see no. 9), has received much attention (see A. J. Le Roux de Lincy, translated and edited by C. Shipman, *Researches concerning Jean Grolier*, 1907, and [H. M. Nixon], *Bookbindings from the Library of Jean Grolier*, 1965). But besides the royal binders such as Pierre and Etienne Roffet (see no. 29) or Claude de Picques (see nos. 23, 24) there were other workshops known at present only from the re-occurrence of certain tools and which are thus usually named or grouped around the first or most famous binding known.

Both in general pattern and in the detailed design of tools French binders of this period were very dependent on Italian models. Some of the earlier bindings displayed patterns made up from small solid tools or fleurons in Italianate patterns, while an outlined inner panel soon became more complex and evolved, under Moorish influence, into the elaborate interlacing or strapwork of the middle of the century. The small tools, mostly sections of arabesque designs, were initially solid but were later made in outline only, the central portion of their surface being sometimes enamelled or painted, and finally were azured (or 'hatched') on the surface. Derived from oriental designs, they were very much part of the decorative idiom of their day and were probably taken from such general artistic books as Francesco Pellegrino's *La Fleur de la Science de Pourtraicture : Patrons de Broderie. Facon arabicque et ytalique* (1530).

22 BOUND BY THE FONTAINEBLEAU BINDER FOR
CATHERINE DE MÉDICIS   Fontainebleau, 1537

Catherine de Médicis married the Dauphin in 1533 and became
Queen on his accession as Henri II in 1547. Catherine's cypher of
two Ks back to back is associated here with the symbols for Dauphiné
and Brittany. Both this and no. 26 appear to have been bound by
the binder working actively in an Italianate style for the Court at
this period and described by Ilse Schunke as the Fontainebleau
binder (see *Bibliothèque d'Humanisme et Renaissance*, XXI (1959),
pp. 603–4). In a forthcoming article, however, Monsieur J. Guignard
suggests that the Fontainebleau binder, as well as the Master of the
Estienne Bible (see no. 41), are in fact part of the workshop of the
Roffet family. These bindings were silver gilt and have, as usual,
oxidized.

On: G. VILLANI, *Croniche . . . nelle quali si tratta dell'origine di Firenze,
e di tutti e fatti e guerra state fatte da Fiorentini nella Italia*, (Vinetia,
per Bartholomeo Zanetti, 1537).
Folio, 320 × 215 × 40 mm. Brown morocco, silver gilt.
Provenance: Gift of Henry, 3rd Baron Coleraine (1693-1749).

CORPUS CHRISTI COLLEGE

23 BOUND BY CLAUDE DE PICQUES FOR JEAN GROLIER
Paris, 1538–48

Bound by Claude de Picques, the French royal binder from 1548,
for the great French bibliophile Jean Grolier (1479?–1565) during
the binder's earlier period when he was using solid decorative tools.
Title and ownership inscription (Grolierii et amicorum) on upper
cover; Grolier's motto (Portio mea domine sit in terra viventium)
on lower.

On: F. BLONDUS, *De Roma triumphante* [and other works], Basileae,
in officina Frobeniana, 1531.
Folio, 347 × 223 × 37 mm. Brown calf, original back, rejointed;
retooled in seventeenth century.
See: BFAC, p. 32; Nixon, *Grolier*, 28 (plate XXVII).
Provenance: Unknown; in All Souls Library by the early eighteenth
century.

ALL SOULS COLLEGE

24 BOUND BY CLAUDE DE PICQUES FOR JEAN GROLIER

Paris, 1538–48

A binding from the period when de Picques was using both solid and open tools. The elaborate double rectangle interlace and some open tools are painted black. Title and ownership inscription on upper cover; motto on lower.

On: M. VIPERA, *De praeclara ac perillustri divini Christianique principatus majestate in Maumetheos libri decem,* (Romae, per Marcellum Silber, 1520).
Folio, 287 × 200 × 24 mm. Brown calf, rebacked.
See: Gibson, 15; Nixon, *Grolier,* 93 (plate LXXXVII).
Provenance: F. Douce (1834).

BODLEIAN (Douce V 255)

25 BOUND FOR ANTOINE DU SAIX

Paris, *c.* 1543

Du Saix was a friend of Rabelais and of Geoffroy Tory and had bibliophilic interests. The inscription on the upper cover, from the Epistle of St. James (Jac. 5. 13) 'Tristatur, quis, vestrum, oret', must be read together with the continuation from Juvenal (Sat. X. 356) on the lower cover, 'Mentem sanam, in corpore, sano'.

On: Horae . . . *ad usum Romanum,* Parisiis, apud Simonem Colinaeum, 1543.
8°, 165 × 105 × 27 mm. Niger morocco with interlacings painted black.
See: J. Porcher, 'Deux livres de la bibliothèque d'Antoine du Saix', *Trésors des bibliothèques de France* IV (1931), pp. 47–51; I. Schunke, 'Der klassische Grolier-Buchbinder in Paris', *Gutenberg Jahrbuch* 1953, p. 166; D. M. Rogers and G. G. Barber, 'A Parisian binding for Antoine du Saix, 1543', forthcoming in *Bodleian Library Record,* VIII, with plate.
Provenance: Painted arms of du Saix on title-page; F. Douce (1834).

BODLEIAN (Douce BB 97)

26 BOUND BY THE FONTAINEBLEAU BINDER FOR CATHERINE DE MÉDICIS

Fontainebleau, *c.* 1535

See the notes to no. 22.

On: *Le dernier volume de l'Ancien Testament,* (Anvers, Martin Lempereur, 1528).

8°, 155 × 95 × 42 mm. Brown morocco, with central panel stained.

Provenance: Early signature 'Mazelin'.

Bodleian (Mason FF 83)

27 BOUND FOR FRANÇOIS I Paris, 1537

The dedication copy presented to François I of France, bound in blue velvet over paste-boards, decorated in gold and silver thread with a border and the royal arms. Until about 1538 many French royal bindings were of velvet, but few others have survived.

On: J. C. P. M. Delphinus, *Mariados,* (Venetiis, in Bernardini de Vitalibus Veneti officina), 1537.

4°, 210 × 150 × 13 mm. Blue velvet, gold and silver thread.

Provenance: Cheffault (seventeenth-century manuscript inscription).

Plate v Astor Deposit (D1)

28 FRENCH PAINTED PANEL-STAMP BINDING Paris? *c.* 1550

The main decoration here is provided by the use of a panel stamp which, with the painted decoration, is typical of the cheaper trade bindings of the period. This style has been traditionally associated with Lyons, but was certainly at least equally common in Paris. The initials AC in the centre are unidentified.

On: [Hebrew Bible containing Numbers, Deuteronomy, Joshua, Judges], Paris, R. Estienne, 1544–46.

12°, 118 × 73 × 35 mm. Brown calf with strapwork painted black.

Provenance: A.C.; E. H. Lawrence; T. R. Buchanan (1941).

Bodleian (Buchanan g.31)

29 FRENCH TRADE BINDING Paris, *c.* 1540

Both the bookstock and binding equipment of the great Parisian bookseller Simon Vostre were bought from his widow in 1523 by

Pierre Roffet and panel-stamped trade bindings of a later period, probably from the shop of Pierre Roffet or his more famous son Etienne, are thus not uncommon on Vostre publications.

On: *Horas de nuestra señora*, Paris, Simon Vostre, [1515?].
    8°, 187 × 117 × 26 mm. Brown calf with parts of the design painted black.
See: Brassington, plate VI.
Provenance: C. Chauncy sale, 1790, no. 2940; F. Douce (1834).

PLATE VI   BODLEIAN (Douce BB 225)

30   BINDING WITH A CAMEO STAMP OF HENRI II
Paris, 1556?

A strapwork binding with open tools and a gilt cameo stamp portrait of Henri II. A number of such cameos are known and several occur on copies of this book. This one is of Dacier's type V (see E. Dacier, 'Les reliures à la médaille d'Henri II', *Trésors des bibliothèques de France*, IV, p. 21).

On: *Coustumes du bailliage de Sens*, Sens, Gilles Richeboys, 1556.
    4°, 230 × 155 × 62 mm. Brown calf with painted strapwork.
See: Brassington, plate XII.

BODLEIAN (Arch. B d.3)

31   BOUND BY THE CUPID'S BOW BINDER FOR JEAN GROLIER
Paris, 1548–54

After de Picques became the royal binder about 1548 Grolier seems to have turned to another binder, called after the most distinctive tool of some of his bindings (but not on any specimen in Oxford) the 'Cupid's Bow binder'. The latest imprint recorded from this shop is 1554. See also no. 33.

On: T. SARAYNA, *De origine et amplitudine civitatis Veronae*, Veronae, ex officina Antonii Putelleti, 1540.
    Folio, 320 × 217 × 20 mm. Brown calf, rebacked.
See: Gibson, 16; Nixon, *Grolier*, 114, plate CVIII.
Provenance: Hibbert sale, March 1829 (7357); Payne & Foss catal., Feb. 1830 (2047); F. Douce (1834).

BODLEIAN (Douce S 528)

Strapwork and open tool binding with cypher of Henri II, the bow associated with Diane de Poitiers, and the motto 'Donec totū impleat orbem', bound by Christopher Plantin, the famous Antwerp printer and bookseller, in the year he fled from Paris. He is known to have produced other bindings for Henri II (see I. Schunke, 'Die Einbände des Christoph Plantin', *Gutenberg Jahrbuch* 1956, pp. 319–30). The bow is similar to that used by Grolier's Cupid's Bow binder whose workshop may have connections with work done later at Antwerp for Marc Lauweryn. For other Plantin bindings see nos. 113 and 118.

On: Horae ad usum Romanum, Parisiis, ex officina Reginaldi Calderii & Claudii eius filii, 1549.
    4°, 230 × 165 × 30 mm. Brown calf, painted, and partly silver gilt; edges gilt and gauffered. Rebacked.
See: Gibson, 22.
Provenance: F. Douce (1834).

PLATE VII   BODLEIAN (Douce BB 184)

Bound in the simpler style of the period with a small onlaid title cartouche. Parts of the decoration were originally speckled. The tools are those of the Cupid's Bow binder (see no. 31).

On: PRISCIANUS, *Prisciani Grammatici . . . libri omnes*, (Venetiis, in aedibus Aldi, et Andreae Asulani soceri, 1527).
    8°, 218 × 136 × 44 mm. Brown calf with red onlay.
Provenance: CVS (initials at head of the upper cover).

                                          MERTON COLLEGE

Both this and the following item are on Books of Hours and bear the name of the respective ladies for whom they were bound. From the very similar general style and the use of the azured tools both would seem to date from shortly after 1545. There is no indication, however, that they come from the same shop nor have their owners been identified. Item 34 has in the centre a version of the 'stirrup' tool often found at this period and a very individual small tool of a bunch of grapes. Marie Mauroy's surname appears on the lower cover.

On: Heures à l'usage de Troyes, Paris, pour Symon Vostre, [1515].
4°, 238 × 159 × 28 mm.
Provenance: Marie Mauroy; C. C. de Bourlamaque; Brooke bequest (1911).

PLATE VIII   KEBLE COLLEGE

35 BOUND FOR MARIE GRYIOLAY   Paris, *c*. 1550

Bound for Marie Gryiolay whose surname appears on the lower cover. See notes to no. 34.

On: Heures à l'usage de Paris, (Paris, veufve de feu Thielman kerver, 1525). 4°, 238 × 170 × 32 mm. Brown calf with red, green, black and white paint. Fore-edge gilt and gauffered.
See: Philip, plate 8.
Provenance: M. Gryiolay; C. Chauncy; F. Douce (1834).

BODLEIAN (Douce BB 170)

36 OFFICIAL BINDING WITH ARMS OF HENRI II
Paris, *c*. 1550

The *Ordre de St. Michel* was instituted by Louis XI in 1469 for thirty-six knights but rapidly outgrew that number. Henri III made it a necessary preliminary step to the *Ordre du Saint Esprit*, whose statutes were also issued, finely bound, to the knights. Both series of bindings are well attested from around 1580 but little is known of the earlier years (see F. Mazerolle, 'Documents sur les relieurs des Ordres royaux de St. Michel et du Saint-Esprit', *Bulletin du bibliophile*, 1895, p. 109 et seq.). The bow, quiver and crescent moon are associated with many bindings for Henri II and below the chain of the order can be seen Saint Michael treading the dragon underfoot.

On: Le livre des statuts & ordonances de l'ordre Sainct Michel, estably par le treschrestien Roy de France Loys unzieme, [Paris? 1550?].
4°, 220 × 150 × 20 mm. Brown morocco.
Provenance: J. Selden (1659).

PLATE IX   BODLEIAN (4° M 21 Jur. Seld.)

25

37 PARISIAN BINDING Paris, *c.* 1550

An unusually simple binding which, apart from some tools similar to, but not identical with, those of Claude de Picques, concentrates its decoration of open tools on the undersized central cartouche. A number of bindings of this type are known on Aldine folios.

On: THEOCRITUS, *Eclogae* [and other works], (Venetiis, characteribus Aldi Manucii, 1495). Hain *15477.
Folio, 321 × 215 × 34 mm. Brown morocco. Edges gilt and gauffered.

ALL SOULS COLLEGE

38 BOUND BY GROLIER'S LAST BINDER Paris, 1555–65

Although, as here, the last binder employed by Grolier used a few open tools, the majority were azured. Also noticeable is the new design now appearing with its emphasis on the centre and corners, the ground being filled with a *semé* of dots.

On: F. FILELFO, *Epistolarum familiarum libri xxxvii*, (Venetiis, ex aedibus Ioannis & Gregorii de Gregoriis fratres [*sic*], 1502).
Folio, 322 × 220 × 40 mm. Brown calf with onlays of olive and citron morocco.
See: Gibson, 18; Nixon, *Grolier*, 131, plate cxxv.
Provenance: C. J. Cisternay du Fay sale, 1725; Count Hoym sale, 1738; Comte de Lauraguais sale, 1770; Duc de la Vallière sale, 1783; J. Dent sale, 1827; Hibbert sale, 1829; Payne & Foss catal., Feb. 1830; F. Douce (1834).

BODLEIAN (Douce P 16)

39 FRENCH BINDING Paris? 1550–60

An all-over strapwork design with a few azured tools and some dotted groundwork in the central area.

On: ARISTOPHANES, *Comoediae novem*, (Venetiis, apud Aldum, 1498). Hain *1656.
Folio, 330 × 220 × 45 mm. Brown calf with strapwork painted black. Covers remounted the wrong way round.
Provenance: Sir William Paddy's bequest, 1613.

ST. JOHN'S COLLEGE

Several bindings are known of around 1550 which were apparently
made without large figured tools. Some have coloured onlays and
some a dotted ground. Mahieu owned a number which G. D.
Hobson (*Maioli*, p. 40) has listed as Group IV, the 'Dotted Group'.
This binding shows all these characteristics as well as an interesting
flat back and certain aspects of the 'Greek' style imported largely
through Venice. Typical are the raised headcaps and the thick
wooden boards grooved round the edges. Several bindings in this
style were commissioned in Paris by the Fugger family about the
same date.

On: Novum Testamentum [in Greek], Lutetiae, ex officina Roberti
Stephani, 1546.
16°, 132 × 84 × 4 mm. Dark brown morocco with light citron
onlay.

PLATE X   BALLIOL COLLEGE

41   BOUND BY THE BINDER OF THE ESTIENNE BIBLE
Paris, *c.* 1540

The large open tool used twice in the centre of the design, together
with a solid tool, are also used on another binding ascribed by Ilse
Schunke to the 'Binder of the Estienne Bible', whose major work
was a folio of 1538 bound for François I (see *Bibliothèque d'Humanisme
et Renaissance*, XXI (1959), p. 599). The initials have not been
identified. See also the notes to no. 22.

On: Hours, Latin and French, manuscript written in France soon
after 1473.
128 × 90 × 35 mm. Brown calf. Gilt edges.
Provenance: DPX; Anthoyne Berbonsier; Knox Ward; R. Rawlinson
(1755).

PLATE XI   BODLEIAN (MS. Rawl. liturg. f.16)

42   PLAIN STRAPWORK BINDING   Paris, *c.* 1555

The elaborate and flowing strapwork ending in outlined flourishes,
and all probably made up from simple curving tools, recalls the

work of the master gilder of Hobson's Maioli Group V, who probably operated in the late 1550s, and that of later Grolier bindings.

On: [E. Vico], *Omnium Caesarum verissimae imagines ex antiquis numismatis desumptae,* ed. 2a, [Parma], Aeneas Vicus, 1553.
 4°, 225 × 160 × 20 mm. Olive morocco.
Provenance: E. Jollyves, Paris, 1628; De Villamblin; F. Douce (1834).

BODLEIAN (Douce V 193)

43 BOUND FOR COUNT VON MANSFELT   Paris, 1556

Peter Ernst von Mansfelt was held prisoner by the French at Vincennes from 1552 to 1557 but in the last months of his captivity, after the death of his first wife, he was allowed more comfortable conditions. In 1557 he returned to the Emperor's service. A small number of Parisian bindings bearing his arms (Mansfelt-Quernfort, here also quartering Heidrungen and Ardnaim) and his motto are known and were presumably bound in 1555 or 1556; this volume is dated 1556 on the spine. Some resemble books by Hobson's Maioli binder VI and a book bound for Mansfelt's captor, Anne de Montmorency, Constable of France.

On: J. LE FÉRON, *Le simbol armorial des armoiries de France, & d'Escoce, & de Lorraine,* Paris, Maurice Menier, 1555.
 4°, 234 × 164 × 18 mm. Brown calf. Edges gilt and gauffered.
See: BFAC, p. 48; J. J. Wild, *Bookbinding in the Library of All Souls College* (1880).
Provenance: 'Car: Linden' in an early hand.

PLATE XII   ALL SOULS COLLEGE

44 STRAPWORK PANEL BINDING   Lyons? *c.* 1550

A coloured strapwork panel binding improved with azured tools. The spine decoration is run horizontally as on many bindings of this kind found on small format Lyonese publications. Formerly the property of Nicolas Joseph Foucault (1643–1721), a number of whose books came to the Bodleian through Richard Rawlinson.

On: *Hore ad usum Romanum*, [Paris], Jo. de Prato, [*c.* 1488]. Proctor 8044.

8°, 150 × 100 × 28 mm. Brown calf.

Provenance: Drouyneau de Thouars; N. J. Foucault.

BODLEIAN (Arch. B f.38)

BINDINGS FOR THOMAS WOTTON

Thomas Wotton (1521–1587), a Kentish squire, was the son of Sir Edward Wotton, Treasurer of Calais, and father of Sir Henry Wotton, Provost of Eton. The more elaborate bindings, notable for their painted strapwork, in his library were collected in his youth, probably before 1553 when he was imprisoned by Queen Mary; his later bindings are undoubtedly of English workmanship and are decorated only with armorial stamps. Where the elaborate ones were bound has been a matter of controversy; the late Lt.-Col. W. E. Moss, whose working collections on bookbinding history came to the Bodleian in 1953, was convinced they were the work of a Canterbury craftsman (*The English Grolier; life, lineage and library of Thomas Wotton*, privately printed, 1941–52), but Mr. Nixon has shown (*Twelve*, pp. 36–48; *Broxbourne*, pp. 64–66, 70–72) that they are almost certainly the work of various Parisian binderies, and has classified them into groups. Examples of the four main types of elaborate bindings are displayed, but none from the simple, and later, armorial groups (though there is one in the Bodleian (Douce D 228) and another on an unrecorded copy of Sir John Cheke's *The hurt of sedition*, 1569, at Christ Church). Most of Wotton's books descended through one female line to the Earls of Chesterfield, who moved them from Kent to Derbyshire in 1747, and eventually to the 5th Earl of Carnarvon, who sent them to the auction room in April 1919, while quite a number went through another female line to Lord Stanhope. However, with the exception of nos. 48 and 57, all the Oxford examples of Wotton bindings were received by gift or bequest long before 1919 and Colonel Moss has shown that these volumes can generally be connected with the families of Wotton's descendants, through whom a few must have escaped. The Wotton books at Exeter College were presented in 1567, twenty years before Sir Thomas's death; it is possible that Wotton had to dispose of part of his library when in trouble during the reign of Queen Mary.

45 BOUND FOR THOMAS WOTTON   Paris, *c.* 1545

This elaborate type of design is one of the commonest found on bindings with Thomas Wotton's ownership inscription stamped on each cover in the centre of an interlacing pattern and belongs to Mr. Nixon's Group I, all apparently bound between 1543 and 1546. Comparison with others in this group has revealed that two finishers, sharing a common stock of tools but not working side by side, were employed; an example of the other man's work can be seen at no. 48.

On: C. JULIUS CAESAR, *Rerum ab se gestarum commentarii*, Parisiis, ex officina Michaelis Vascosani, 1543.
Folio, 350 × 226 × 40 mm. Brown calf, original back.
See: BFAC, no. L. 22; Moss, no. 28; Nixon, *Twelve*, pp. 38–41.
Provenance: Thomas Wotton; John Fitzwilliam; bequeathed by him, 1699.

MAGDALEN COLLEGE

46, 47, 49   BOUND BY A WOTTON BINDER   Paris, *c.* 1549

The tools on this variously patterned set belong to Mr. Nixon's Group IIA, most of which have more rectilinear designs than two of those displayed. It is not absolutely certain that Wotton owned these books as neither his inscription nor his arms are present, although this may be due to the fact that there was no space for such additions if the set was acquired already bound. Since these volumes form part of a collection of the Fathers, presented in 1567, which includes the St. Augustine (nos. 54, 56) bearing Wotton's armorial stamp, it is not perhaps unreasonable to assume a common ownership.

On: ST. JEROME, *Opera*, 8 tom. in 3 vols., Parisiis, ex officina Carolae Guillard, 1546.
Folio, 385 × 260 × 60 (70, 68) mm. Brown calf, rebacked.
See: Moss, nos 66–69; Nixon, *Twelve*, p. 41.
Provenance: Sir William Petre (1502?–72); presented by him, 1567.

PLATES XIII–XV   EXETER COLLEGE

48   BOUND FOR THOMAS WOTTON   Paris, *c.* 1545

This Cicero was once part of a set of at least seven volumes, each stamped with Wotton's ownership inscription and each with a varying design of black interlacing ribbon combined with floral tools. It belongs to the same group as no. 45, but is an example of the work of the other finisher in this particular shop.

31

On: M. T. Cicero, *Epistolae familiares*, Parisiis, ex officina Roberti Stephani, 1543.
8°, 175 × 105 × 35 mm. Brown calf, original back.
See: Maggs Bros. Ltd., Catal. 500, 1928, no. 198; Friends of the Bodleian, *Eighth annual report 1932–33*, pp. 5, 10; Moss, no. 32; Nixon, *Twelve*, pp. 38–40; Nixon, *Broxbourne*, p. 66.
Provenance: Thomas Wotton; Maggs Bros. Ltd.; J. H. Burn; presented by him, 1932.

BODLEIAN (Don. e.28)

49   See nos. **46, 47**.

50   BOUND BY A WOTTON BINDER   Paris, *c.* 1551

Another example of the group of bindings to which the set of St. Jerome belongs (nos. 46, 47, 49); the use of straight lines in the design, favoured by this finisher, is very noticeable. Where and how Francis Douce acquired his Wotton bindings (see nos. 51, 53, 55, 58) is uncertain. It is possible that after the bulk went to Derbyshire in 1747 part of Wotton's library remained in Kent where Douce, whose family had connections with Malling, somehow found them.

On: B. Rhenanus, *Rerum Germanicarum libri tres*, Basileae, (ex officina Ioannis Oporini, 1551).
Folio, 306 × 198 × 55 mm. Brown calf, rebacked.
See: Moss, no. 100; Philip, plate 11; Nixon, *Twelve*, p. 41.
Provenance: F. Douce (1834).

BODLEIAN (Douce R 213)

51   BOUND FOR THOMAS WOTTON   Paris, *c.* 1550

Besides books (see no. 50), Francis Douce also owned several detached covers from volumes bound for Wotton. The two mounted here belong to the same group as nos. 46, 47, 49, 50 and the rectilinear pattern can be seen to resemble the last greatly. The rather irregular position of the armorial cartouche in the centre suggests that it may be an addition rather than an integral part of the design.

On: Detached book cover.
  220 × 152 mm. Brown calf.
See: Brassington, pp. 20–21 (plate x); Moss, no. 111; Nixon,
  Twelve, pp. 41–42.
Provenance: Thomas Wotton; F. Douce (1834).

BODLEIAN (Douce Bindings A 33)

52 BOUND BY A WOTTON BINDER   Paris, *c.* 1552

The tools used here are the same as those on nos. 46, 47, 49–51,
while there are also similarities in the design. No definite connection
with Wotton has been traced. The spine is early eighteenth-century
work, when the book was rebound entirely.

On: M. VITRUVIUS POLLIO, *De architectura*, Lugduni, apud Ioan.
  Tornaesium, 1552.
  4°, 240 × 155 × 30 mm. Light brown calf, rebacked.
See: Moss, no. 107; Nixon, *Twelve*, pp. 41–42.
Provenance: Edmund Granger; presented by him, 1705.

EXETER COLLEGE

53 BOUND BY A WOTTON BINDER   Paris, *c.* 1550

Another example of the work of the same binder as nos. 46, 47, 49–52.
There is again no sign of ownership by Wotton, but the central
cartouche has a quatrefoil design which would have prevented the
addition of an armorial stamp. In view of the fact that Douce, the
only definite owner, also possessed authentic Wotton books, it is
perhaps not too rash to ascribe the same pedigree in this case.

On: Detached book cover.
  295 × 185 mm. Brown calf.
See: Brassington, pp. 22–23 (plate xi); Moss, no. 112; Nixon,
  Twelve, pp. 41–42.
Provenance: F. Douce (1834).

BODLEIAN (Douce Bindings A 31)

The tools and curvilinear design show that this was bound in the same shop as no. 50. There is a larger proportion of azured tools, mostly rather large, while the open tools tend to be narrow and pinched-looking compared with the very similar ones used on nos. 46, 47, 49–53. Each of the eight volumes in this set of St. Augustine has a different design, five permitting the addition of Wotton's arms. All have been rebacked twice.

On: St. Augustine, *Opera*, Basileae, ex officina Frob., 1542.
  Folio, 360 × 240 × 75 (85) mm. Brown calf.
See: Moss, nos. 36–43; Nixon, *Twelve*, pp. 41–42.
Provenance: Thomas Wotton; Sir William Petre (1502?–72); presented by him in 1567.

Exeter College

55 BOUND BY A WOTTON BINDER   Paris, *c.* 1550

Another example of work from the same shop as nos. 54 and 65.

On: S. Grynaeus, *Novus orbis regionum ac insularum*, Basileae, apud Io. Hervagium, 1537.
  Folio, 305 × 200 × 52 mm. Brown calf, rebacked.
See: Moss, no. 7; Philip, plate 10; Nixon, *Twelve*, pp. 41–42.
Provenance: F. Douce (1834).

Bodleian (Douce G 300)

56 See no. **54.**

57 BOUND FOR THOMAS WOTTON   Paris, *c.* 1552

A number of books with the date '1552' stamped in the centre of each cover can be traced to Thomas Wotton's library. Though the style is similar to those of the two groups in nos. 45–56, these dated volumes came from another workshop, one of whose distinctive tools is the large trefoil with an azured 'shadow' behind it, seen here flanking the date. This binding was unknown to Lt.-Col. Moss, but it is interesting that Wotton owned another copy of this book by John Bale, bearing his armorial stamp.

On: J. BALE, *Illustrium maioris Britanniae Scriptorum Summarium*, (Gippeswici, per Ioannem Overton [really Wesel, D. van den Straten], 1548).
    4°, 208 × 156 × 35 mm. Brown calf, original back.
See: Hobson, *English*, no. 8; Moss, no. 79; Nixon, *Twelve*, pp. 42–43.
Provenance: Thomas Wotton; James Bindley (1737–1818).

PLATE XVI   ASTOR DEPOSIT (D3)

58 BOUND FOR THOMAS WOTTON   Paris, *c.* 1582

Another example of a '1552' Wotton binding from the same workshop as no. 57, though no tool is common to both specimens. Like nos. 51 and 53, it comes from the bequest of Francis Douce.

On: Detached book cover.
    307 × 192 mm. Brown calf.
See: Moss, no. 113; Nixon, *Twelve*, pp. 42–43.
Provenance: Thomas Wotton; F. Douce (1834).

                                   BODLEIAN (Douce Bindings A 34)

59 BOUND FOR THOMAS WOTTON   England? *c.* 1546

Besides his elaborately decorated books, Thomas Wotton also owned some simply bound in several styles, such as the one shown here. The armorial stamp may be an addition. It is not certain whether this group was bound in England or France; only three examples are known, all small and easily carried to Paris.

On: C. P. SENARCLAEUS, *Historia vera de morte J. Diazii*, [Basle, J. Oporinus], 1546.
    8°, 160 × 95 × 22 mm. Brown calf.
See: Moss, no. 70; Nixon, *Twelve*, p. 47.
Provenance: Thomas Wotton; George Coningsby; bequeathed by him, 1766.

                                          BALLIOL COLLEGE

Five books are known with Wotton's ownership inscription dated
1548 stamped on the covers. Two, of which this is one, have medallions of Plato and Dido while the others have Tarquin (or Mars) and
Lucretia. These bindings were probably executed in England, though
there is no conclusive evidence, while the fact that this particular
volume was printed in Paris might point to France. Note the brass
guards and clasps, obscuring parts of the inscription, possibly added
when the book was rebacked.

On: A. Osiander, *Harmoniae Evangelicae libri IIII*, Lutetiae, ex
officina Rob. Stephani, 1545.
12°, 132 × 67 × 32 mm. Brown calf, rebacked.
See: Moss, no. 59; Nixon, *Twelve*, p. 47.
Provenance: Thomas Wotton; in the Bodleian Catalogue of 1738, but
not in that of 1674.

Bodleian (8° T 102 Th.)

ENGLISH COLLECTORS OF THE EARLIER
SIXTEENTH CENTURY

The most noticeable feature of binding during the first half of the sixteenth century in England was the introduction of gold-tooling, which, after one still-born attempt about 1519 (no. 63), began to be used about 1530, but did not become at all common before the death of Henry VIII in 1547. Many books in the royal libraries were so decorated and specimens from the reign of Henry VIII to that of Mary I are shown, while titled men (nos. 71, 73, 75) and women (no. 72), cardinals (nos. 61, 63), an academic (no. 69), and a merchant (no. 74) are also represented. The books displayed were all bound in England, with the exception of nos. 72 and 73 which came from France and Italy respectively, and, as there was as yet no real native style, the indebtedness to European fashions is obvious.

61 BOUND BY KING HENRY'S BINDER   London, *c.* 1530

The volume displayed is a typical example from what is probably the earliest group of gold-tooled bindings executed in England. The style shows Italian influence, while tools like the flame and knot in the central circle, for instance, were also popular in that country. But both styles and tools are based directly on the French gilt bindings of the 1520s, which were themselves close copies of Italian models. Over twenty volumes from the same shop, called 'King Henry's binder' by G. D. Hobson, are known, all probably bound before 1535; the one shown here was possibly bound during Cardinal Reginald Pole's stay in England between 1527 and 1532. The blind-tooled inner roll can also be seen on no. 64, though there are no smaller tools common to both.

On: Catena on Isaiah, Greek manuscript written by Bernardino Sandro of Cremona in the early sixteenth century.

  332 × 230 × 70 mm. Brown calf over wooden boards, rebacked.
See: Hobson, *Cambridge*, pp. 66–67 (plate xxii); Philip, plate 3; J. B. Oldham, *English blind-stamped bindings*, 1952, Roll R.P. *a.* 1; H. M. Nixon, 'Early English gold-tooled bookbindings',

Studi di bibliografia e di storia in onore di Tammaro de Marinis, III, 1964, pp. 289–91.
Provenance: Cardinal Reginald Pole; presented by him, 1557.

NEW COLLEGE (MS. 41)

62 BOUND BY THE GREENWICH BINDER   London, *c.* 1545

Among the books bequeathed by its founder, Sir Thomas Pope, to Trinity College in 1555 are four with 'Ex grenewech' written on their title-pages; three are in white buckskin, like the one displayed, while the fourth (no. 67) is in brown calf. These volumes, formerly in the Royal Palace at Greenwich, were probably supplied by Thomas Berthelet, the King's Printer. At one time it was thought that Berthelet included a bindery in his printing works, but Mr. Nixon has demonstrated that in fact books in this group were bound in different shops, and calls the binder of the volume displayed the 'Greenwich binder'. The royal shield is made up of small tools. The edges of the leaves are inscribed in gilt 'Rex in aeternum vive', found on all three buckskin volumes at Trinity, on a similarly bound book in Chetham's Library, Manchester, and on an embroidered binding in the British Museum.

On: A. BROICKWY, *In quatuor Evangelia enarrationes*. Coloniae, apud Petrum Quentell, 1539.
Folio, 337 × 210 × 55 mm. White buckskin.
See: Book Collector, IV (1955), p. 236; [H. M. Nixon], *Royal English bookbindings in the British Museum*, 1957, p. 4; H. M. Nixon, 'Early English gold-tooled bookbindings', *Studi di bibliografia e di storia in onore di Tammaro de Marinis*, III, 1964, pp. 300–2 (plate v).
Provenance: Greenwich Palace; Sir Thomas Pope; bequeathed by him, 1555.

TRINITY COLLEGE

63 THE EARLIEST ENGLISH GOLD-TOOLED BINDING
England, *c.* 1519

The volume displayed contains a manuscript of Richard Whitinton's presented to Cardinal Wolsey not later than 1519. The blocks representing St. George slaying the dragon and the Tudor royal emblems were obviously not designed for this binding, since they are placed sideways across the covers, and were possibly intended for use with some other form of leather-work. It is believed that the blocks used were wooden. Gold can be made to adhere to leather without the use of heat by glairing in the usual way and leaving the covers and blocks in a press for some hours. This early example did not start a fashion for gold-tooling, which only began to be used in the 1530s and did not become common until the 1550s.

On: R. WHITINTON, Latin epigrams addressed to Cardinal Wolsey, manuscript written *c.* 1519.
    240 × 160 × 13 mm. Brown calf.
See: Brassington, pp. 14–15 (plate VII); Paris, Bibliothèque Nationale, *Le livre anglais*, 1951, no. 389; Nixon, *Broxbourne*, p. 119; H. M. Nixon, 'The gilt binding of the Whitinton *Epigrams*, MS. Bodley 523', *The Library*, 5th series, VII (1952), pp. 120–1; H. M. Nixon, 'Early English gold-tooled book-bindings', *Studi di bibliografia e di storia in onore di Tammaro de Marinis*, III, 1964, pp. 286–7. Elements from this binding design were used on the binding of the Folio Society's edition of George Cavendish, *Thomas Wolsey* (1962).
Provenance: Cardinal Thomas Wolsey; reached the Bodleian between 1603 and 1605.

BODLEIAN (MS. Bodley 523)

64 BOUND BY KING HENRY'S BINDER   London, *c.* 1530

These two covers, collected by Francis Douce, were bound in the same shop as no. 61. A characteristic feature is that while the rolls are in blind, the small tools are in gilt.

On: Detached book covers.
    149 × 157 mm.
See: Gibson, no. 20; Hobson, *Cambridge*, pp. 66–67; J. B. Oldham, *English blind-stamped bindings* (1952), Roll R.P. *a.*1; H. M. Nixon, 'Early English gold-tooled bookbindings', *Studi di bibliografia e di storia in onore di Tammaro de Marinis*, III, 1964, pp. 289–91.
Provenance: F. Douce (1834).

BODLEIAN (Douce Bindings A 30)

D
39

65 BOUND BY THE MEDALLION BINDER   England, *c.* 1545

The style of this binding is similar to several others added to the royal libraries during the reign of Edward VI, though there are no initials on this unrecorded example. The tools are associated with a binder who worked from the end of Henry VIII's reign to the early years of Elizabeth I, and may possibly be the same as King Henry's binder (nos. 61, 64), since some tools are common to both although a decade separates their work. As in no. 62, the royal shield is again made up of small individual pieces.

On: EUSEBIUS Pamphili, *Evangelicae praeparationes*, Lutetiae, ex officina Rob. Stephani, 1544.
Folio, 352 × 230 × 65 mm. Dark brown calf, original back.

See: Hobson, *Cambridge*, pp. 74–81; Nixon, *Twelve*, pp. 1–2 (plate 1); Baltimore, no. 347; *Book Collector*, XII (1963), p. 60; H. M. Nixon, 'Early English gold-tooled bookbindings', *Studi di bibliografia e di storia in onore di Tammaro de Marinis*, III, 1964, pp. 291–4.

Provenance: Henry Cole; presented by him while Dean of St. Paul's, 1556–60.

PLATE XVII   ST. JOHN'S COLLEGE

66 BOUND FOR HENRY VIII BY THE FLAMBOYANT BINDER
England, 1545

The bindings on four books presented to Henry VIII during the last years of his reign, all associated with Wouter Deleen (Galterus Deloenus), denizened in 1539 and a member of the Royal Household, are profusely decorated with rather coarse tools, suggesting a Teutonic exuberance and determination to include the maximum amount of gold possible. There is also a long inscription, beginning on the upper cover: HENRY THE VIII. BY THE GRACE OF GOD KYNG OF ENGLAND. FRAVNCE. AND IRELANDE. AND. C. WITH GODES. HELP. ANO. D. M.D.XLV. and continuing on the lower: O. IESV. MISERERE. MEI. DVM. TEMPVS. EST. MISERENDI. WIVAT. REX. AMEN. Only one other of the four recorded books has a long inscription.

On: HERMAN, Archbishop of Cologne, *Ein Christliche in dem Wort Gottes gegrünte Reformation* [&c.], (Bon, durch Laurentium von der Müllen, 1543), preceded by a letter of Wouter Deleen to

King Henry VIII offering this book and sending a Latin version of selected parts.

Folio, 307 × 200 × 40 mm. Brown calf, original back.

See: Philip, plate 5; Worshipful Company of Goldsmiths *and* the Oxford Society, *Treasures of Oxford; catalogue of the exhibits* (1953), no. 195 (plate 38); Nixon, *Twelve,* p. 8; H. M. Nixon, 'Early English gold-tooled bookbindings', *Studi di bibliografia e di storia in onore di Tammaro de Marinis,* III, 1964, pp. 298–300; *Book Collector,* XIV (1965), p. 200.

Provenance: Wouter Deleen; Henry VIII.

NEW COLLEGE (MS. 136)

67 BOUND FOR HENRY VIII England, *c.* 1545

This volume, like no. 62, is inscribed 'Ex grenewich' and was probably acquired by Sir Thomas Pope while winding up Henry VIII's estate. It is, however, the work of a different binder from the other Greenwich books. This shop had the royal shield all on one tool and at least two sorts of crown. The inscription round the edge is also characteristic. The other type of crown can be seen on a copy of J. L. Vives, *Very fruteful instruction of a Christen woman* (1541) at Christ Church. G. D. Hobson separated the work from this shop into two—King Edward's binder and Queen Mary's binder—but Mr. Nixon has proved there could only have been one on account of the combination of tools found, so that it is now known as the King Edward and Queen Mary bindery. The inscription on the upper cover reads: LEX PER MOYSEM DATA EST GRATIA ET VERITAS PER IHESVM CHRISTVM FACTA EST, and on the lower, AD NOSTRAM DOCTRINAM SCRIPTA SVNT QVECUNQVE ENIM SCRIPTA SVNT. The edges of the leaves have been painted with a floral frame surrounding REX and HENRICVS on the upper and fore-edges, but that on the lower edge has been worn away.

On: OECUMENIUS, *Expositiones ex diversis sanctorum patrum commentariis ab Oecumenio et Aretha collectae,* Veronae, (apud Stephanum & fratres Sabios), 1532.

Folio, 456 × 232 × 96 mm. Brown calf, original back.

See: Hobson, *Cambridge,* pp. 76–79; *Book Collector,* I (1952), p. 244; II (1953), p. 272; [H. M. Nixon], *Royal English bookbindings in the British Museum,* 1957, p. 4 (plate 3); H. M. Nixon, 'Early

41

English gold-tooled bookbindings', *Studi di bibliografia e di storia in onore di Tammaro de Marinis*, III, 1964, pp. 295–8.
Provenance: Henry VIII; Sir Thomas Pope; bequeathed by him, 1555.

PLATE XVIII TRINITY COLLEGE

68 BOUND FOR QUEEN MARY I England, *c.* 1546

Another example of the work of the King Edward and Queen Mary binder, here in white leather. The same tools can be seen in the corners as, for instance, in no. 67, while there is again an inscription, here 'QVÆSTVS MAGNVS PIETAS'. Both covers are decorated in the same way; the single 'M' in each central shield may indicate that the book was bound for Mary before her accession.

On: ARNOBIUS, *Disputationes adversus gentes*, Basileae, (apud Hier. Frobenium et Nic. Episcopium), 1546.
8°, 170 × 110 × 36 mm. White leather, original back.
See: references to no. 67.
Provenance: Mary I; John Stott, 1662.

MERTON COLLEGE

69 BOUND BY THE KING EDWARD AND QUEEN MARY BINDER England, *c.* 1551

These two smaller books show some typical less elaborate bindings made for ordinary persons rather than monarchs. The 'W.B.' on one of them possibly stands for William Bill, Master of Trinity College, Cambridge (d. 1561); while on its companion a space has been left in the shield for initials should they be required. The floral corner-piece tool can be seen also at the outer corners of the made-up cartouche around the royal arms on no. 67, while the tools used in the shield here are also used on no. 68.

On: (a) G. CONTARENO, *La republica e i magistrati di Vinegia*, Vinegia, Baldo Sabini, 1551.
8°, 157 × 100 × 28 mm. Dark brown calf.

(b) Polybius, *Polibio historico greco tradotto per L. Domenichi*, Vinegia, Gabriel Giolito, 1546.

8°, 165 × 103 × 37 mm. Dark brown calf.

See: References to no. 67, and Hobson, *English*, p. 14 (plate 12).

Provenance: Francis Harewell; presented by him, 1615.

BODLEIAN (8° C 98 Art.; 8° P 73 Art.)

70 POSSIBLY BOUND BY JOHN DE PLANCHE

London, *c.* 1572

The binding displayed is an early example of the use in England of blocked centre- and corner-pieces with arabesque designs, similar to work then coming from French, and especially Lyonese, craftsmen. The flat spine with broad bands of ornament also shows Lyonese influence. The raised metal lions' heads are made of silver. By means of a close study of the tools, Mr. Nixon has linked this volume to a group of fine bindings made for Matthew Parker, Robert Dudley, and other men prominent in their day. A distinctive feature of a number of these bindings, not present here, is an L-shaped corner-piece decorated with trophies and including the initials 'IDP'. These may stand for John de Planche, a French binder working in London from about 1567. No. 126 and a 1583 Bible at Trinity College can also be ascribed to the same shop, as well as a Welsh New Testament bound for Elizabeth I now in the Landesbibliothek at Dresden. The last has the same tools used in a similar pattern for the foliate design joining the centre-piece to the outer border in the volume shown here (see I. Schunke, 'Ein Dresdner Einband des Elizabethanischen Buchbinders John de Planche', *Gutenberg Jahrbuch* 1958, pp. 320–1).

On: W. Forrest, History of Joseph; a poem, manuscript of first part only, *c.* 1569.

330 × 235 × 50 mm. Brown calf on wooden boards; rebacked, original spine laid down.

See: R. W. Hunt, 'The manuscript collection of University College, Oxford', *Bodleian Library Record*, III (1951), pp. 22–23; *Book Collector*, XIII (1964), p. 340.

Provenance: Charles Theyer; presented by him, *c.* 1700.

UNIVERSITY COLLEGE (MS. 88)

Robert Dudley, Earl of Leicester, was one of several Elizabethan noblemen whose books were sumptuously bound. Over seventy have survived and another example is shown later (no. 75). The bear and ragged staff badge has a crescent for cadency, indicating a second son, and since Robert Dudley, born a fifth son, did not become the second surviving son until 1557 these bindings were presumably made after that date, although many of the books were printed earlier. The style is reminiscent of French bindings of the period and is the work of a man styled the' Dudley binder', whose fount of tools closely resembled that of the 'Morocco binder', employed by Archbishop Parker (see nos. 118–19).

On: J. XIPHILINUS, *Dionis Nicaei rerum Romanarum epitome,* Lutetiae, ex officina Roberti Stephani, 1551.
Folio, 261 × 165 × 30 mm. Brown calf, original back.
See: Brassington, pp. 26–27 (plate XIII); W. E. Moss, *Bindings from the library of Robt. Dudley, Earl of Leicester, 1533–1588* (1934), no. 33 (plate 10); Hobson, *English,* p. 188; Baltimore, 352; *Book Collector,* VIII (1959), p. 282; H. M. Nixon, 'Early English gold-tooled bookbindings', *Studi di bibliografia e di storia in onore di Tammaro de Marinis,* III, 1964, p. 305.
Provenance: Robert Dudley, Earl of Leicester; J. Selden (1659).

BODLEIAN (AA 15 Med. Seld.)

72 A FRENCH BINDING FOR MILDRED CECIL
France, *c.* 1552

This typical mid-sixteenth-century French binding of tooled strapwork on a stippled background was formerly owned by Mildred (1524?–89), daughter of Sir Anthony Cooke, who became the second wife of William Cecil, first Lord Burghley. The style is reminiscent of Thomas Wotton's bindings. A noted Greek scholar, she was wont to write her name in Greek characters in her books, as she has done on the one displayed.

On: APOLLINARIUS, *Interpretatio Psalmorum, versibus heroicis* [in Greek],

Parisiis, apud Adr. Turnebum, 1552.

8°, 175 × 110 × 18 mm. Brown calf, original back.

Provenance: Mildred Cecil; George Coningsby; bequeathed by him, 1766.

BALLIOL COLLEGE

73 BOUND FOR SIR WILLIAM PICKERING   Italy, *c.* 1550

Sir William Pickering (1516–75), a Yorkshire Protestant country gentleman and diplomat, was also a bibliophile, but in spite of having been ambassador in Paris, 1550–52, he did not own elaborately decorated bindings like his friend and executor, Thomas Wotton (nos. 45–60). Instead, he merely added to the covers his armorial stamp, of which there are four varieties. Since these different stamps were used concurrently, as on the volumes displayed, they do not indicate the growth of his library, from which about forty books are now known. The traces of ties on the upper and lower edges of the covers, together with the small circles in the corners, suggest an Italian origin for the bindings shown here. Like Wotton, Pickering fell into disfavour during Mary's reign; his daughter Hester married Edward Wotton, son of Thomas, so the libraries of the two friends descended together to the Earls of Chesterfield.

On: F. JOSEPHUS, *De l'antichità giudaiche. Tradotto per M. Pietro Lauro Modense*, 2 vols., Vinegia, Baldassar Constantini, 1549.

8°, 162 × 103 × 38 (35) mm. Dark brown calf, rebacked.

See: Sotheby's, 5 Mar. 1937, lot 873 (illus.); Moss, p. ix; I. G. Philip, 'Sir William Pickering and his books', *Book Collector*, V (1956), p. 234; Baltimore, no. 281.

Provenance: Sir William Pickering; Hester Wotton; Earls of Chesterfield; W. E. Moss; purchased 1951.

BODLEIAN (Vet. F 1 f. 59, 60)

74 BOUND FOR JOHN CROUCHMAN   England, *c.* 1550

This is another example of the work of the King Edward and Queen Mary binder (see nos. 67, 69). The initials and merchant's mark in the centre of the cover stand for John Crouchman, Mercer, whose signature is on the title-page; a similarly bound volume is in Lambeth

45

Palace Library. The interlacing, stippling and decoration are reminiscent of contemporary French workmanship.

On: W. TYNDALE, *The practyse of prelates*, Marborch, [H. Luft], 1530.
8°, 147 × 100 × 22 mm. Brown calf, rebacked.
See: References to no. 67.
Provenance: Unknown; in Corpus before the end of the nineteenth century.

CORPUS CHRISTI COLLEGE

75 BOUND FOR ROBERT DUDLEY   England, *c.* 1567

Another of the eight variant stamps of the bear and ragged staff badge found on bindings made for Robert Dudley, Earl of Leicester (see no. 71). The style resembles that of no. 70, but on a smaller scale; both the covers have a background of trefoils with corner-pieces while the spine is similarly divided into alternate panels of trefoils and floral designs. The tools used here are not found on any other known Dudley binding, but since the book was produced under the auspices of Archbishop Matthew Parker, it may be the work of one of the craftsmen who bound for the latter. This binding has not been previously described.

On: AELFRIC, *A testimonie of antiquitie*, London, John Day, [1567].
8°, 157 × 90 × 17 mm. Brown calf, original back.
Provenance: Anthony Smyth; Richard Peter; acquired in 1769 by Richard Gough (1809).

BODLEIAN (Gough Sax. lit. 127)

46

FRENCH BINDINGS OF THE LATER
SIXTEENTH CENTURY

While rectilinear and curvilinear strapwork bindings were still much in fashion around the middle of the century, the earlier solid tools gave way to, first, open tools which could, like the strapwork, be painted or enamelled, then to azured tools. As the number and variety of tools increased there evolved from the 1560s to 1640s the fanfare style, so called after an imitation binding of the early nineteenth century made for Charles Nodier on a collection of fanfare scores. Here the strapwork, bounded on one side by two lines and on the other by one, forms a series of regular compartments all over the book covers, the central compartment often bearing the owner's arms or name, but also not infrequently left empty. The spaces are filled with a number of small tools, including particularly palmettes and volutes, and sprays of foliage (see G. D. Hobson, *La reliure à la fanfare*, 1935). Another style belonging to the 1590s was that associated with Pietro Duodo, the Venetian ambassador to France from 1594 to 1597, where the surface of the book is covered by a uniform series of leafy ovals, each containing a naturalistic flower. The regularity of these also slightly recalls the *semé* style which was, both with and without centre- and corner-pieces, increasingly coming into favour at the same period.

76 BOUND FOR CARDINAL DE GRANVELLE   Paris, *c.* 1584

Antoine Perrenot de Granvelle, Archbishop of Malines (1517–86), virtual master of the Low Countries in the years before 1564 and then Viceroy of Naples, was a great collector ever since his student days with Bembo in Italy. He commissioned manuscript copies, translations (as he knew no Greek), and bindings both from Italy (see no. 2) and from France.

This binding belongs to the second group of bindings executed for Granvelle in Paris and is almost identical with that of a Dion Cassius copied out for him in 1548 (see M. Piquard, 'Les livres du Cardinal de Granvelle à la Bibliothèque de Besançon', *Trésors des bibliothèques de France*, VI, pp. 16–29 and plate v). The Emperor Charles V had allowed Granvelle's father, who was his chancellor, to add the crowned two-headed eagle to the family arms.

On: Apollodorus, Bibliotheca, manuscript of the fifteenth century, in Greek.

340 × 230 × 20 mm. Brown calf.

See: Philip, plate 7.

Provenance: de Granvelle; J. P. D'Orville; J. C. Banks; purchased 1804.

Bodleian (MS. D'Orville 1)

77 BY CLAUDE DE PICQUES FOR THOMAS MAHIEU

Paris, *c.* 1550

Thomas Mahieu, or Maioli if he was really an Italian by birth, was secretary to Catherine de Médicis and later, like Grolier, one of the Treasurers of France. He was the second great French private book collector and his bindings have been studied by G. D. Hobson in his *Maioli, Canevari and others* (1926). He collected actively from at least 1549 to 1565. Like Grolier, whom he apparently knew, he had the title of the book and the ownership inscription THO. MAIOLII ET AMICORUM lettered on the upper cover and his motto or monogram on the lower. Mahieu's mottoes were 'Ingratis servire nefas' (It is a terrible thing to serve ungrateful masters) and 'Inimici mei mea mihi non me mihi' (My enemies may rob me of my goods, but not my soul).

An almost identical binding owned by Mahieu, also on a book printed at Venice in 1478, is discussed by Mr. Nixon in *Twelve books*, pp. 19–21. Both have flat spines, the edges gilt and gauffered with the knotwork in the Italian style, and are tooled on an unusual leather with a background pattern of small flames in outline. The use of patterned leather seems to have been rare although de Thou owned some bindings done over a more elaborately marbled leather. There are two other books formerly owned by Mahieu in the Bodleian, a 1543 Horace (fol. △ 125), recorded by Hobson as no. 41 (Group VII) and a manuscript of Phile written by Angelus Vergecius in Paris in 1564 (MS. Auct. F 4.16).

On: Lactantius, *De divinis institutionibus*, (Veneciis, Andreas de Paltasichis & Boninus de Boninis, 1478). Hain *9813.

Folio, 290 × 190 × 45 mm. Brown calf.

See: Hobson, *Cambridge*, p. 84; Nixon, *Twelve*, pp. 19–21; Philip, plate 6.

Provenance: T. Mahieu; early inscriptions 'Adiuva me domine et salvus ero', 'Deus in nomine tuo Salvum me fac', 'Dirupisti Dñe vincula mea'; acquired by the Bodleian in 1697 from the widow of Edward Bernard, Savilian Professor of astronomy.

BODLEIAN (Auct. N 4.11)

78 BOUND BY ONE OF MAIOLI'S BINDERS   Paris, *c.* 1550

Both by general style and by some particular tools this binding seems to be associated with Hobson's Maioli Group I, or 'Aesop' group. Its flat spine with contemporary lettering and endpapers with the name of Simeon Nivelle, papermaker to the University of Paris, also assure its French origin.

On: G. VALVERDE, *Anatomia del corpo humano*, Roma, per Añt. Salamanca et Antonio Cafreri, 1560.
Folio, 314 × 212 × 41 mm. Olive green morocco.
See: J. J. Wild, *Bookbinding in the library of All Souls College* (1880); BFAC, plate 23; Hobson, *Maioli*, p. 38.

PLATE XIX   ALL SOULS COLLEGE

79 BOUND FOR PHILIBERT DU CHATELET   Paris, *c.* 1545

A rectilinear strapwork design similar to a number of Grolier bindings and with tools close to, but different from, those of Claude de Picques. Presumably, from the inscriptions and illuminated text, a wedding gift for Philibert du Chatelet (1511–99, motto: Ung pour jamais) and Marguerite de Doncourt (name on lower cover with the motto: Unne pour le tout).

On: Heures à l'usaige de Rome, Paris, pour Simō Vostre, [1501?].
8°, 228 × 141 × 25 mm. Olive calf. Rebacked.
See: Philip, plate 6.
Provenance: P. du Chatelet; F. Douce (1834).

BODLEIAN (Douce L subt. 53)

80 BOUND BY CLAUDE DE PICQUES Paris, *c.* 1550

A rectlinear strapwork binding, outlined in black, and with azured tools including, top and bottom, de Picques's characteristic two-lobed tool. The interlocked ovals are found on a number of bindings at this period. Like no. 77 the book has a flat spine.

On: R. Estienne, *Hebraea, Chaldaea, Graeca et Latina nomina virorum in Bibliis,* Parisiis, ex officina Roberti Stephani, 1537.
8°, 172 × 115 × 30 mm. Brown calf. Edges gilt and gauffered.

Balliol College

81 BY THE BINDER OF GROLIER'S CUSPIANUS
Paris, *c.* 1545

A rectilinear strapwork and open tool binding by the binder of Grolier's *Cuspianus* (1540) which is in a style similar to that of the 'Fuggermeister' and to the shop responsible for Group II of Wotton's bindings. An inscription, possibly MIDARCE, has been erased from the centres of both covers. A very similar binding with some identical tools is found on a Colines *Horae* of 1543 (see Wilmerding sale, 5 March 1951, item 184).

On: J. Gagny, *Brevissima & facillima in omnes divi Pauli epistolas . . . scholia,* Parisiis, apud Simoneum Colinaeum, 1543.
8°, 172 × 115 × 30 mm. Brown calf. Edges gilt and gauffered.
Provenance: 'Menion'; Jesuit college at Caen; Mrs. Gorman, 1891.

Keble College

82 TRANSITIONAL EARLY FANFARE BINDING Paris, 1568?

The open tools, fairly open ornamentation without foliage, coloured strapwork and raised bands of the spine suggest that this book was bound in 1568 at the beginning of the fanfare period. It bears the name and, on the title-page, the painted arms of S[oeur] Magdalene Sanguin (1590–1670), head of the convent at Senlis founded by her brother, the Bishop, but these would seem to be later additions. The Sanguin family were related to the de Thous (see no. 84). René Benoist's original French translation of the Bible, published in 1566, had been condemned in 1567 by the Sorbonne since he had relied on the Geneva Bible. Benoist, who was confessor to Mary Queen of Scots and to Henri IV, later retracted.

On: *La Sainte Bible* [Latin and French], 2 vols., Paris, chez Sébastien Nivelle, 1568.
Folio, 260 × 170 × 67 mm. Brown calf with parts of the design painted black, red, and silver. Edges gilt and gauffered.
See: Philip, plate 14.
Provenance: Magdalene Sanguin; F. Douce (1834).

BODLEIAN (Douce BB 199)

83 FANFARE BINDING FOR JAMES VI   Paris, *c.* 1601

One of four volumes evidently commissioned specially for James VI, presumably before 24 March 1603 when he became King of England. The two known extant volumes are the same in general design but differ in the details. Volume three of the set, in the collections of King George V, was recorded in Hobson's *Fanfares*, no. 175 and the coloured frontispiece. Another ornate binding, apparently with several identical tools, on an *Orlando furioso* of 1573, was illustrated in C. J. Sawyer's catalogue 91 (1928), plate 7. This particular form of the royal arms is otherwise unrecorded.

On: R. BELLARMINE, *Disputationum de controversiis Christianae fidei, adversus huius temporis haereticos opus,* tom. I, Ingolstadii, ex typographia Adami Sartorii, 1601.
Folio, 352 × 225 × 55 mm. Red morocco.
Provenance: James I.

ASTOR DEPOSIT (D8)

84 FANFARE BINDING WITH THE ARMS OF J. A. DE THOU
Paris, 1584

Jacques Auguste de Thou was one of the main early collectors of fanfare bindings. Up to his first marriage in 1587, after which his bindings bore only his arms, he is known to have possessed twenty in this style whereas only thirteen are recorded for Henri III. Most of the fanfares are of the early style, bear his arms as a bachelor and a particular angel's-head tool. Hobson, who records the present binding as no. 142, argues that though it comes, like most of the others, from the 'atelier de la première palette', the absence of the angel's-head tool and the existence of a very similar binding on another copy of this work suggests that they were bound for a bookseller who sold one to de Thou, whose arms were then added. In any case the binding illustrates well the developed style with palmettes, volutes and classical trophies. The latter were particularly popular at the time and engravings of them were published by Enea Vico, the engraver and publisher of no. 42, and J. Androuet du Cerceau.

On: G. SALUSTE DU BARTAS, *La seconde semaine ou Enfance du monde,* Paris, P. L'Huillier, [1584].
4°, 240 × 160 × 35 mm. Olive green morocco.
See: Brassington, plate XVIII; Hobson, *Fanfares,* Appendice B, 'Les reliures à la fanfare de J. A. de Thou'.
Provenance: J. A. de Thou.

BODLEIAN (Arch. B d.4)

85 BOOKS FROM THE LIBRARY OF J. A. DE THOU
Paris, mostly before 1617

Jacques Auguste de Thou (1553–1617), a contemporary of Sir Thomas Bodley, was, like the latter, a statesman and book collector. Premier Président du Parlement de Paris and partly responsible for drafting the Edict of Nantes, he travelled and thus bought, amongst other things, works straight from the press in Antwerp and Venice. The manuscript catalogue of his library, made just after his death, lists over six thousand books and manuscripts. This library was kept together at his express desire and only finally broken up (together with the Rohan–Soubise library into which it was incorporated in 1706) the year before the French Revolution. In its early years it was to some extent a 'public library' open to scholars and considerably added to and in 1644 Louis Jacob referred to it as 'le Parnasse des Muses'. It is also interesting to note that de Thou owned a copy of the first Bodleian catalogue (1605; de Thou's copy exhibited here).

Before his first marriage in 1587 de Thou collected many fine fanfare bindings (see no. 84). Other books, however, had only a plain binding, some vellum as shown here, but the majority were bound in red or olive morocco with his arms on the covers and his initials (IADT) on the spine. It should be noted nevertheless that this plain style appears also to have been used for some additions to the library made after his death. In 1584 he married Marie de Barbançon Cany, whereon the sequence of fine bindings ceases, the armorial stamp shows both shields, and the monogram changes to IAM (Jacques Auguste, Marie). Shortly after her death in 1601 he married Gasparde de La Chastre; the armorial stamp was changed again and the monogram became IAG. A final de Thou armorial stamp was cut around 1651 for Jacques Auguste de Thou II when he became Comte de Meslay-le-Vidam. The shelfmarks of the de Thou (or, possibly, of the Rohan–Soubise) library are still written in many of the books, and, in some cases, on the upper covers as well.

The various armorial stamps and binding styles are all illustrated here by some of the hundred de Thou library books known to be in the Bodleian.

These books are exhibited in the large case at the end of the exhibition.

LATE FANFARE STYLE BINDINGS   Paris, c. 1600

Both these bindings, while retaining the characteristic fanfare double and single line strapwork and either the large spiral or the small tailed volute, tools which are found as late as the middle 1620s, are evidently strongly influenced by the predominant European 'centre and corner' style.

86 *On:* Hours for the use of Paris, French fifteenth-century manuscript.
   160 × 102 × 35 mm. Brown morocco.
Provenance: R. Gough (1809).

                        BODLEIAN (MS. Gough liturg. 12)

87 *On: Novum Testamentum* [in Greek], Lutetiae, ex officina Roberti Stephani, 1549.
   12°, 120 × 80 × 42 mm. Red morocco.
Provenance: Early shelfmark J.5.39; J. S. Mill; presented by Miss Helen Taylor, 1905.

PLATE XX   SOMERVILLE COLLEGE

88 MIDDLE PERIOD FANFARE   Paris, 1595

The use of numerous small flower tools, four different kinds of foliage and the dove of the Holy Ghost (only used after 1578 when the Ordre du Saint Esprit was founded) argue that this was a contemporary binding produced at least before 1610. One of the publishers, Georges Drobet, was *relieur du roy* in the early 1590s and died in 1596. Although illiterate, Drobet is recorded as having signed one binding, an unusual practice at this time (see Hobson, *French*, p. 63). Another binding possibly by him is shown as no. 102 (plate XXIII).

On: L'Office de la Vierge Marie, Paris, pour Jamet Mettayer, Jehan Houzé; et George [*sic*] Drobet, 1595.
8°, 182 × 111 × 42 mm. Olive morocco.
Provenance: C. Fielin; Madame Ailain?; F. Douce (1834).

BODLEIAN (Douce BB 217)

89 MIDDLE PERIOD FANFARE   Paris, *c.* 1590

The profusion of small flowers again suggests the middle fanfare period. A very similar binding, on an Italian book of 1567, was illustrated in Coulet et Faure's Catalogue 67 (1961) as item 8. The Breviary exhibited here is of a hitherto unknown use.

On: Breviarium incliti monasterij sancte crucis beati Leufredi [La-Croix–St. Leufroy] *Ebroiceñ. Diocesis impensis reverendi . . . Nicolai Hebert, eiusdē monasterii abbatis*, Parisiis, per Desiderium Mahieu, [1544].
8°, 155 × 102 × 33 mm. Light brown morocco.
Provenance: The library founded by Bishops John Vertue (1826–1900) and J. B. Cahill (1841–1910); purchased at Christies', 5 July 1967, lot 125.

BODLEIAN (Arch. B f.58)

90 LATE FANFARE BINDING   Swiss? *c.* 1590

The reduced number of floral or symbolic tools together with the regular alternate horizontal and vertical hatching on the edges of the boards show that this belongs to the later fanfare period. The pear tool is unusual. The title-page bears the signature of Jacques Couet du Vivier, a convert to Calvinism, who was either in Scotland or Switzerland, with a few short visits to Nancy, from 1572 until his death at Basle in 1608, when the book passed to his son Jacques II.

54

On: Novum Testamentum, T. Beza interprete, [Geneva, H. Estienne], 1580.

8°, 195 × 120 × 60 mm. Olive morocco.

Provenance: Jacques Couet du Vivier, I and II; presented by L. M. Earlty.

WORCESTER COLLEGE

91 FANFARE BINDING   Paris, *c.* 1590

The bird and marguerite tools date from the 1580s but the treatment of the edges of the boards is of a later date. The initials D and M being found both separately and interlaced suggest that this was a marriage binding.

On: Hours according to the use of Treguier and a Dominican Processional as used in the convent of the nuns of St. Louis at Poissy, manuscript written in France in the sixteenth century. 160 × 107 × 35 mm. Brown calf.

Provenance: Initials D.M.; N. J. Foucault; R. Rawlinson (1755).

BODLEIAN (MS. Rawl. liturg. f.35)

BOUND FOR PIETRO DUODO   Paris, *c.* 1595

This style of all-over decoration with leafy roundels containing well-cut naturalistic flowers is usually associated with the name of Pietro Duodo, the Venetian ambassador to Paris between 1594 and 1597 who is thought to have had all the little books which formed his travelling library bound there in this style. His books, which on account of the marguerite found on some were formerly attributed to Marguerite de Valois, bear his arms and the motto 'Expectata non eludet' (She whom I await will not escape me). Different coloured leathers were possibly used to denote the subjects of the books.

92 *On:* F. PETRARCH, [Works], Venetia, Giorgio Angelieri, 1586. 16°, 123 × 75 × 43 mm. Light brown morocco.

Provenance: P. Duodo; Mary Berry; H. H. Milman; purchased 1952.

BODLEIAN (Arch. B f.53)

E   55

93 *On:* HIPPOCRATES, [Works in Greek and Latin], 2 vols., Francofurdi, apud haeredes Andreae Wecheli Claudium Marnium & Ioann. Aubrium, 1587.

16°, 125 × 80 × 35 mm. Light brown morocco.
Provenance: P. Duodo; R. S. Turner.

94 *On:* T. TASSO, *Rime e prose*, Ferrara, Giulio Vasalini, 1589.

16°, 133 × 74 × 46 mm. Light brown morocco.
Provenance: P. Duodo.

95 DUODO STYLE BINDING Paris, 1597?

A Duodo style of binding with armorial central oval showing a tower and the motto 'Ad ipsam curre'. Manuscript notes inside the volume record family events up to 1596 and suggest that its owners were the De Salviac de Vielcastel. A member of this family, Jean, married in 1597 and the Breviary may have been bound on that occasion. The motto comes from Proverbs 18.10.

On: Breviarium secundum usum insignis ecclesie collegiate beate Marie Virginis de Belna [Beaune] *Eduensis dyocesis,* (in inclita civitate Gebenēsi per Jacobū vivien, 1517). Bohatta 1997.

8°, 160 × 100 × 50 mm. Light brown morocco.
Provenance: De Salviac de Vielcastel; Hailstone sale 1891; Brooke bequest (1911).

PLATE XXI   KEBLE COLLEGE

96 BOUND FOR MARIE DE SENICOURT IN THE DUODO STYLE Paris, 1595

The owner's name appears in the central medallion, divided between the upper and lower covers. She has inscribed the book 'Monsieur Dupre mon cousin curé de Percy m'a doné ceste paire d'heure en l'an 1595' on the title-page. The religious symbols introduced here are never found on real Duodo bindings.

On: Hours, French provincial manuscript of the late fifteenth century. 150 × 102 × 31 mm. Olive green morocco.

Provenance: Marie de Senicourt; Mme Lefebure; M. Laurens 'advocat au Parlement, de Crespy en Valois'; d'Elincourt; A. Papeguy 1836.

ASTOR DEPOSIT (A19)

DUODO STYLE BINDINGS   Paris, *c.* 1600

Again numerous religious emblems have here been combined with naturalistic flowers on one of which a butterfly is carefully poised.

97 *On:* Hours, Paris, illuminated by the workshop of the Master of the Duke of Bedford, *c.* 1450.
210 × 140 × 42 mm. Olive morocco.
Provenance: Bought from Pearson's, 1904.

ASTOR DEPOSIT (A13)

98 *On:* Hours, written for Claude de Lorraine, first Duc de Guise, 1527.
120 × 75 × 22 mm. Dark olive morocco.
Provenance: Claude de L'Aubespine, secretary of the Ordre du Saint Esprit 1579–1608 (see the initials on the covers, with the C on the lower cover, and the emblem of the Saint Esprit); 'Bibl. Duchesse de Berry', no. 19; Brooke bequest (1911).

KEBLE COLLEGE (MS. 44)

99 ANIMAL TOOLS BINDING   France, *c.* 1600

A remarkable binding with eleven pairs (both left- and right-facing) of animal tools as well as a butterfly, floral and other tools. Though sixteenth-century in inspiration the border at the top and bottom belongs stylistically to the next century.

On: [Hours according to the use of Rouen, Rouen, 1518].
12°, 167 × 90 × 30 mm. Brown calf.
Provenance: Initials on spine BHX; N. J. Foucault; Mlle de Théville; R. Rawlinson (1755).

BODLEIAN (8° Rawl. 1108)

100 BINDING WITH *S FERMÉ* Paris, *c.* 1600

Bound in a mixture of the Duodo and the centre- and corner-piece styles with a number of religious symbols including the *S fermé* used on bindings from about 1580 and probably signifying *fermesse* or loyalty.

The owner of the initials CDL has not been identified.

On: [Hours for the use of Paris], [Paris], Jehan Poitevin, (1498). Proctor 8363.
8°, 160 × 102 × 27 mm. Red morocco.
See: Hobson, *Fanfare*, no. 282.
Provenance: CDL; R. Rawlinson (1755).

PLATE XXII BODLEIAN (8° Rawl. 1096)

CONTINENTAL LATER SIXTEENTH-CENTURY BINDINGS

While Paris and the Italian towns still provided much of the best binding of this period many fine bindings now began to come from other areas. The geographical position of Lyons and the importance of its book trade naturally made it a centre of great activity but in many cases it has been impossible to tell whether some of the finer bindings came from there or from the Calvinist stronghold of Geneva to which the printer Robert Estienne had fled in 1550. A number of binders from Lyons are also known to have emigrated to London where certain aspects of Lyonese style are to be found (see no. 70). German binders, like Jacob Krause, also produced much fine work but unfortunately no really representative specimens have been found in Oxford. Some collectors in the Low Countries had patronized Parisian binders from earlier on but the flight of Christopher Plantin, who was originally a bookbinder, from Paris in 1549 also helped to encourage a high standard of bookbinding in Antwerp.

101 CENTRE- AND CORNER-PIECE BINDING   Paris, *c.* 1585

Centre- and corner-piece binding with a *semé* of small fleurs-de-lys and an elaborate outside border.

On: G. AUDEBERTUS, *Parthenope*, Parisiis, apud Jacobum du-Puys, 1585.
4°, 282 × 210 × 14 mm. Limp vellum.
Provenance: J. Brodeau 1633.

ALL SOULS COLLEGE

102 BINDING POSSIBLY BY GEORGES DROBET   Paris, 1587?

A diaper binding with emblems from the arms of the Lorraine family, probably for Claude, the illegitimate son of Charles, Duc de Guise, who was Abbot of St. Nicaise-de-Reims and later of Cluny and who died in 1612. The sword-hilts and rosettes on the diapers have led the binding to be associated with a group attributed to Georges Drobet (see also no. 88). All-over symbolic bindings were not uncommon at this date.

On: *Missale romanum*, Antverpiae, ex officina Christophori Plantini,
    1587.
    Folio, 355 × 225 × 45 mm. Dark brown sheep.
See: BFAC, plate LXV; Hobson, *French*, p. 63.
Provenance: Claude de Guise; T. R. Buchanan (1941).

PLATE XXIII   BODLEIAN (Buchanan c.6)

103 ROYAL DEDICATION BINDING   Paris, 1572

Semé binding with fleurs-de-lys and initial H. Arms in centre.
Presentation copy with manuscript dedication to the then Duc
d'Anjou, later Henri III, foreseeing that he would become a 'roi
chenu' [white-haired with old age].

On: P. VIRGILIUS MARO, *Aeneidos, & in eum commentarii Iacobi Heliae*
    Marchiani, Parisiis, ex typographia Dionysii a Prato, 1572.
    4°, 226 × 167 × 10 mm. Vellum.
Provenance: Henri III; 'Feillie doct. Sorbon'.

                                             ALL SOULS COLLEGE

104 *SEMÉ* BINDING   French, *c.* 1600

A *semé* binding covered with a form of Lorraine cross. A very similar
binding on a book printed at Basle in 1554 is shown in Gilhofer's
catalogue 180, item 423. For other bindings for members of the Lorraine family see nos. 102, 201, 205. H. W. Chandler (1828–89) was
Waynflete Professor of Moral and Metaphysical Philosophy, a
curator of the Bodleian, and the bibliographer of the *Nicomachean Ethics*.

On: ARISTOTLE, *Ad filium Nicomachum de vita & moribus libri x, A. V.*
    Strigelio nunc iterum editi, Francoforti, 1583.
    12°, 162 × 100 × 43 mm. Brown calf.
Provenance: Ex libris Chartres; H. W. Chandler; presented by Mrs.
    M. S. Evans, 1889.

                                             PEMBROKE COLLEGE

Centre- and corner-piece binding with *semé* field and a tool of unusual design, similar versions of which also occur on books associated with Lyons and dating between 1568 and 1579. The design of this tool is probably of Italian origin. The central cartouche bears the unidentified initials T.A.

On: HELIODORUS, *Historia Aethiopica*, Basileae, ex officina Hervagiana, 1534.
4°, 218 × 150 × 20 mm. Black morocco.
Provenance: T.A.; 'de Ponsainpierre du Peron . . . Praesidialium Academici Lugdunensis'.

QUEEN'S COLLEGE

106   ARMORIAL CORNER-PIECE BINDING   Lyons? *c.* 1590

A corner-piece binding with a *semé* of small flowers to match those on the armorial stamp, itself surrounded by more flowers. The arms have not been identified but may be those of Vernecour if the date following the signature on the title-page is to be read as 1588. The horizontal decoration of the spine would suggest that the binding came from Lyons or Germany.

On: M. A. MURETUS, *Variorum lectionum libri xv*, Antwerpeae, apud Christophorum Plantinum, 1586.
8°, 176 × 112 × 37 mm. Brown calf.
Provenance: P. Vernecour; 'Barat 1659'.

ALL SOULS COLLEGE

107   PRESENTATION BINDING BY THE 'KING'S BOOKBINDER'   Geneva, 1588

Another copy of this edition of the Bible was bound in a very superior style for presentation to Henri de Navarre but by the time it reached Paris he had become a Catholic and it was returned to Geneva. The same binder appears to have been responsible for a number of other pieces, including the volume exhibited here with onlaid English royal arms (see G. D. Hobson, 'Une reliure aux armes d'Henri III', in *Trésors des bibliothèques de France*, III, pp. 149–59, and I. Schunke,

Die Einbände der Palatina (1962), I, pp. 227–30). The fore-edges of the volumes are decorated in the typical Genevan style.

On: La Sainte Bible, à Genève, 1588.
   Folio, 430 × 290 × 100 mm. Brown calf. Rebacked.
Provenance: Unknown; in the Bodleian by 1675.

BODLEIAN (A 5. 10 Th.)

108 BOUND BY THE 'KING'S BOOKBINDER'   Geneva, 1572

Another binding by the 'King's bookbinder' (see no. 107), this time with an inset, cameo-style, lion's face.

On: H. ESTIENNE, *Thesaurus linguae Graecae*, tomus III (IV) [Geneva], H. Estienne, 1572.
   Folio, 400 × 245 × 90 mm. Brown calf.
Provenance: T. Turner, President, bequeathed in 1714.

PLATE XXIV   CORPUS CHRISTI COLLEGE

109 BOUND BY THE 'GOLDAST MASTER'   Geneva, *c.* 1580

A typical example of the plain style of binding produced by the Geneva binder who worked for the historian Melchior Goldast (see I. Schunke, *Die Einbände der Palatina* (1962), I, pp. 222–6).

On: EURIPIDES, *Tragoediae octodecim*, Basileae, per Ioannem Hervagium, 1551.
8°, 193 × 120 × 50 mm. Brown calf, rebacked.
Provenance: Archbishop Laud (1634).

ST. JOHN'S COLLEGE

110 BOUND BY THE 'KING'S BOOKBINDER'   Geneva, *c.* 1580

Another binding by the 'King's bookbinder' (see nos. 107, 108), this time in a plainer style but still typical, with its combination of a border of azured tools with oval central stamp, of Genevan and German work.

On: A. Caninius, *Institutiones linguae Syriacae, Assyriacae . . . Addita est . . . Novi Testamenti multorum locorum historica enarratio,* Parisiis, apud Carolum Stephanum, 1554.
4°, 225 × 148 × 20 mm. Brown calf.
Provenance: Archbishop Laud (1634).

Plate xxv   St. John's College

111 SUNKEN PANEL BINDING   Lyons or Geneva, 1580

The sunken (or Venetian style) panel is achieved by the use of a second board to form the outer frame. An almost identical binding is recorded on another copy of this work.

On: T. de Bèze, *Psalmorum sacrorum libri quinque vario carminum genere Latine expressi,* 2a ed., Genevae, 1580.
8°, 180 × 110 × 38 mm. Brown calf; the sunken panel of green calf with silver paint.
Provenance: Unknown, but in the Bodleian before 1605.

Bodleian (8° B 7 Th.)

112 BOUND FOR HECTOR LE BRETON   Paris, *c.* 1600

Hector Le Breton held a series of posts at court between 1590 and 1621 and in 1644 published a paraphrase of the Book of Proverbs in French verse. A number of books bound for him are known and all those in red morocco bear his arms, name, and titles like the present example (see Hobson, *French,* p. 74).

On: J. Scohier, *L'estat et comportement des armes,* Bruxelles, chez Iean Mommart, 1597.
Folio, 305 × 200 × 16 mm. Red morocco.
Provenance: A. Thistlethwayte; bequeathed by him 1771.

Wadham College

113 BOUND BY CHRISTOPHER PLANTIN   Antwerp, *c.* 1555

Christopher Plantin (1520–89), the famous Antwerp printer and bookseller, started life as a bookbinder and throughout his career seems to have had connections with the trade. Although Plantin was

63

influenced by French models, a detailed tool study allows a distinct corpus of work to be attributed to his bindery. This particular binding, like that on the J. Schöner, *Opera mathematica* (Nuremberg, 1551), in Exeter College Library, has not previously been recorded. For a Plantinian binding probably executed in Paris see no. 32.

On: A. BRUCIOLI, *Nuovo commento ne divini et celesti libri evangelici*, tom. 4 [–7 in one], Vinetia, (Francesco Brucioli, & ei frategli, 1544).
Folio, 320 × 210 × 82 mm. Brown calf.
See: G. Colin, 'A propos d'une reliure de Plantin', *Studi di bibliografia e di storia in onore di Tammaro de Marinis*, II, 1964, pp. 1–14.

MAGDALEN COLLEGE

114 PRESENTATION BINDING FOR PHILIP II OF SPAIN
Bruges? 1563

Presented by Hubert Goltzius (1526–83), the painter and numismatist, to Philip II who appointed him historiographer royal. A number of Goltzius's presentation bindings are known (see I. Schunke, *Der Einbände der Palatina* (1962), I, pp. 248–9) and some are from the same bindery as books bound for Marc Lauweryn, Seigneur de Watervliet, a rich citizen of Bruges and patron of Goltzius (see Goldschmidt, pp. 282–4).

On: H. GOLTZIUS, *C. Iulius Caesar sive historiae imperatorum Caesarumque Romanorum ex antiquis numismatibus restitutae liber*, Brugis Flandrorum, (apud Hubertum Goltzium, 1563).
Folio, 336 × 227 × 45 mm. Red calf.
Provenance: Philip II; J. Boucher (1738–1804); F. Douce (1834).

BODLEIAN (Douce G subt. 6)

115 GERMAN PIERCED VELLUM BINDING
Schmalkalden, 1593

Cut or pierced vellum bindings showing coloured silk underneath were produced in Germany and Holland around 1600. This binding is one of a small series known, all on copies of this book and possibly the work of the Schmalkalden binder Hans Bapest von Erfurt (see Nixon, *Broxbourne*, pp. 105–7). The arms on the upper cover are

64

those of the translator Maurice the Learned, Landgrave Hesse of (1572–1632). The Bodleian possesses another pierced vellum binding on a Dutch *album amicorum* of *c.* 1612 (MS. Rawl. B. 4).

On: Davidis Psalterium, vario genere carminis Latine redditum ab Mauritio Hassiae Landgravio, Smalcaldiae, (Michael Schmück, 1593).
8°, 181 × 150 × 28 mm. Pierced vellum over green silk. Edges gilt and gauffered.
Provenance: Several inscriptions for 1595, possibly by Urban von Boersburgh(?); Augustus Frederick, Duke of Sussex.

BODLEIAN (4° A 111 Th. BS.)

116 BOUND FOR J. E. VON MESPELBRUNN Würzburg, 1586

Most of the bindings in the library of Julius Echter von Mespelbrunn, Prince-Bishop of Würzburg (1573–1617), were of typical sixteenth-century plain German pigskin decorated with blind tool rolls. However, they often bore an armorial stamp in the centre which was brightly painted. At least two versions of the stamp exist, one round, one square, the latter being used both with and without a special square border. Another characteristic of his library was that the fore-edges of the books were often lettered, sometimes with his name.

The Prince-Bishop's library, which was looted by the Swedes in 1631, also contained one of the most extraordinary sixteenth-century bindings and apparently the only round one known. Five works were bound together, the inlaid pages forming a circle (see G. D. Hobson, 'German Renaissance patrons of bookbinding', *Book Collector*, IV (1954), pp. 171–89, and, for the round binding, J. R. Abbey Sale, 1965, no. 336 and plate 37).

On: JACOBUS DE VITRIACO, *Sermones*, Antverpiae, in aedibus viduae & haeredum Ioannis Stelsii, 1575.
Folio, 340 × 270 × 75 mm. White pigskin.
Provenance: Von Mespelbrunn; T. Clayton, presented 1680.

MERTON COLLEGE
This item is exhibited in the large case at the end of the exhibition.

117 GILT PANEL BINDING Germany? *c.* 1552

Except for its gilding this binding recalls the strong earlier German style of blind-stamped binding. A later owner, Isbrant Willemsen, has had his name tooled over that of the original owner which is now illegible.

On: Le Nouveau Testament, [Paris], Robert Étienne, 1552.
  12°, 147 × 92 × 60 mm. Brown calf, rebacked.
Provenance: Orisio? Geral??; I. Willemsen.

MANCHESTER COLLEGE

118 BOUND BY CHRISTOPHER PLANTIN   Antwerp, 1553

Plantin's workshop seems to have produced bindings in a number of different styles as can be seen by comparing the several Plantinian bindings known on copies of this book. Some of these were produced for Cardinal de Granvelle, the Duc de Croy, and Cardinal Ercole Gonzaga. Part of the design is painted, part stippled. The initials RI were added after the original binding but their owner has not been identified.

On: [O. DE LA MARCHE], *El cavallero determinado*, Anvers, Iuan Steelsio, 1553.
  4°, 223 × 155 × 25 mm. Brown calf, edges gilt.
Provenance: R.I.; presented in 1653 by W. Carpender of Christ Church, later White's Professor of Moral Philosophy.

BODLEIAN (4° A 7 Art. BS.)

119 PRESENTATION BINDING FOR QUEEN MARY
                                    Germany, 1555

German silver-gilt binding, now tarnished, in earlier traditional blind-tooled style. Stamped 'Maria Regina Angliae' and dedicated to Philip and Mary.

On: J. SLOTANUS, *De retinenda fide orthodoxa et catholica adversus haereses et sectas, et praecipue Lutheranam*, Coloniae, Ioannes Novesianus, 1555.
  4°, 203 × 142 × 32 mm. Brown calf.
Provenance: Queen Mary; early college inscription.

NEW COLLEGE

66

ENGLISH BINDING IN THE REIGNS OF ELIZABETH I AND JAMES I

During the reign of Queen Elizabeth I, gold-tooling slowly became more common in Britain; there was as yet no real national style and patterns followed continental fashions, while the workmanship tended towards coarseness. Centre- and corner-piece designs, often on fields of small tools, began to supplant the use of interlaces, while the number of owners who stamped their coats of arms on book covers grew. The nobility began to patronize native craftsmen (nos. 120–1, 125, 130, 132), as did those who commissioned presentation copies (nos. 122, 131), and also private persons or institutions for special volumes (nos. 123–4, 127–9). Possible Scottish and Huguenot bindings (nos. 124, 133) are also displayed here.

120 BOUND FOR MATTHEW PARKER, ARCHBISHOP OF CANTERBURY London, *c.* 1570

Matthew Parker was one of the outstanding collectors of books and manuscripts of his day; although much of what he left is now in Cambridge libraries or at Lambeth Palace, several of his books are found in Oxford. In 1573 at least there were binders working for him in Lambeth Palace, but what was actually done there is a matter for speculation. The tools used on Parker's own books and presentation copies are also found on bindings for other people, so it is most likely he employed the best craftsmen available who occasionally worked within the Palace itself. The centre- and corner-piece style is based on French models; the cornucopia blocks in the corners were popular in Paris *c.* 1570–80, though used in England until about 1630.

Other volumes bound for Archbishop Parker, from the same shop, include a Matthew Paris (1571) at All Souls, a companion to the book displayed, and *Huloets Dictionarie* (1572) in the Bodleian (H 4.10 Art.). The same tools are also found on a folio Bible of 1568 at Trinity, painted with the arms of Richard Stoneley, of Ingatestone, Essex, and his wife, Anne Branche; on John Bernard, *Oratio* (1568) with the Tudor royal arms, among Lord Astor's books deposited in the Bodleian; on John Day, *Booke of Christian prayers* (1590) at Keble; on the All Souls Benefactors' Register, bound

1605–06; and on Daniel Featley, *The Romish fisher caught* (1624) with Archbishop Abbot's arms, at Manchester College.

On: MATTHEW of Westminster, *De rebus Britannicis*, Londini, ex officina Thomae Marshii, 1570.
Folio, 304 × 202 × 60 mm. Light brown calf, rebacked with original spine pasted on.

See: Hobson, *Cambridge*, pp. 96–97, plate XXXV; Hobson, *English*, pp. 16, 26; *Book Collector*, VI (1957), pp. 278, 386; XIII (1964), p. 340.

Provenance: Matthew Parker, Archbishop of Canterbury; John Parker; presented by him, 1602.

PLATE XXVI   ALL SOULS COLLEGE

121 BOUND FOR MATTHEW PARKER, ARCHBISHOP OF CANTERBURY   London, *c.* 1573

The centre-piece with the flower above and below and the corner blocks are the same as those on the Statutes of Corpus Christi College, Cambridge, written and bound for Archbishop Parker in 1573–74, as well as on four books printed by John Day for Parker between 1572 and 1574. It has been suggested that it was this group that was actually bound by the craftsmen known to have worked within Lambeth Palace, in view of the close associations of the books with the Archbishop, but this is not certain.

On: G. ACWORTH, *De visibili romanarchia contra N. Sanderi monarchiam*, Londini, apud Johannem Dayum, 1573.
4°, 220 × 155 × 17 mm. Light brown calf, original back.

See: References to no. 120.

Provenance: Matthew Parker, Archbishop of Canterbury; Bartholomew Clarke, Fellow of King's College, Cambridge (d. 1590); William Wake, Archbishop of Canterbury; bequeathed by him, 1736.

CHRIST CHURCH

122 BOUND FOR QUEEN ELIZABETH I   London, *c.* 1588

The fine binding of this Welsh Bible was probably made for presentation to Elizabeth I. The block of the royal arms, with the Queen's initials inserted in the cartouche, is rare and only two other examples are recorded. The corner blocks were being used as late as 1625. The volume displayed was originally owned by Anna (1550–1631), fourth wife of Sir Thomas Myddelton, of Chirk, Denbighshire, a notable entrepreneur who financed the publication of the first portable Welsh Bible in 1630. Lady Myddelton gave it in 1634 to one of her step-grandchildren, Sir Thomas Salusbury of Lleweni (1612–43), the poet and Royalist (see W. J. Smith, ed., *Calendar of Salusbury correspondence 1553– c. 1700* (1954), Table Ic, and *Dictionary of Welsh biography* (1959), pp. 676, 902).

On: *Y Beibl*, London, by the Deputies of Christopher Barker, 1588.
　　Folio, 340 × 220 × 70 mm. Light brown calf, rebacked.
See: Nixon, *Broxbourne*, pp. 112–30.
Provenance: Anna, Lady Myddelton; Sir Thomas Salusbury.

CHRIST CHURCH

123　A CENTRE- AND CORNER-PIECE BINDING
England, c. 1570

The style of this binding, with centre- and corner-pieces on a field of small crosses-crosslet, is similar to that found in many parts of Europe in the sixteenth century. The side-pieces are an unusual feature; each is made up of two tools, in one case combining corner-pieces; these last are on a binding for the 7th Earl of Shrewsbury in the Victoria and Albert Museum (see J. P. Harthan, *Bookbindings* (Victoria and Albert Museum illustrated booklet no. 2, 2nd ed. (1961), plate 33).

On: H. HOWARD, Treatise of natural philosophy, manuscript written at Cambridge in 1569.
　　208 × 145 × 25 mm. Light brown calf, original back.
See: Philip, plate 15.
Provenance: Thomas Waine; presented by him, 1735.

BODLEIAN (MS. Bodley 616)

124　POSSIBLY BOUND BY ROBERT LEKPREVIK
Edinburgh? c. 1567

The style of this binding, with its large oval centre-piece, small corner blocks and wide border, all decorated in arabesque, suggests

France rather than Scotland as the country of origin. In view of the contents of the book and the fact that its printer, Robert Lekprevik, is known to have had a bindery between 1561 and 1582, the volume shown may well be an example of his work about 1567, when an early owner wrote his name on an end-leaf. Dr. W. S. Mitchell, however, thinks the binding could date from nearer the turn of the century. At this period, Scottish bookbinding had no really distinctive features and, as in England, followed European fashions.

On: *The forme of prayers and ministration of the sacraments as used in the English Church at Geneva*, Edinburgh, Robert Lekprevik, 1564.
 8°, 150 × 95 × 47 mm. Light brown calf, rebacked.
See: W. S. Mitchell, *A history of Scottish bookbinding, 1432–1650* (1955), pp. 68–69, 123.
Provenance: Signature, dated 13 Aug. 1567, deleted and now illegible; Richard Thomson; presented by him, 1623.

CORPUS CHRISTI COLLEGE

125 BOUND FOR WILLIAM CECIL, LORD BURGHLEY
London, c. 1573

William Cecil, in spite of his involvement in affairs of state, managed to form a choice library, of which a considerable portion was sold by auction in 1687 (see W. Y. Fletcher, *English book collectors* (1902), pp. 38–43). Nearly all his books are decorated with one of three varieties of an armorial stamp, though sometimes he only inscribed his name. Six other examples of this particular stamp, with an 'N' reversed in the motto, are known in Oxford libraries. His second wife, Mildred, was also a book collector (see no. 72). The style of the corner-pieces is very similar to contemporary French designs.

On: L. HUMPHREY, *Ioannis Iuelli Angli vita et mors*, Londini, apud Johannem Dayum, 1573.
 4°, 202 × 147 × 30 mm. Light brown calf, original back.
Provenance: William Cecil, 1st Baron Burghley (1520–98); Nathaniel Crynes; bequeathed by him, 1745.

BALLIOL COLLEGE

POSSIBLY BOUND BY JOHN DE PLANCHE

London, *c.* 1600

The centre-piece is one of the largest English blocks known. Mr. Nixon's study of the tools associated with it on other bindings has shown that it was used in the shop of the 'IDP' binder, possibly John de Planche, a Frenchman working in London from about 1567 (see no. 70). The corner-pieces here are also found on a 1583 Bible in the Chadwyck–Healey collection belonging to Trinity College, which has a different, though also large, centre-piece.

On: Bible in Latin, manuscript written in the thirteenth century. 420 × 260 × 114 mm. Brown calf, original back.
See: C. Davenport, *Royal English bookbindings* (1896), pp. 44–46 and fig. 12; *Book Collector*, XIII (1964), p. 340.
Provenance: Stephen of Cranebrook; Rochester Priory; John Buckeridge (d. 1631); presented by him, 1620.

PLATE XXVII ST. JOHN'S COLLEGE (MS. 4)
This item is exhibited in the large case at the end of the exhibition.

127 BOUND FOR SIR THOMAS BODLEY London, 1604

Sir Thomas Bodley took as great pains with the Benefactors' Register as with all other details of his Library. Unable to find a scribe whose handwriting satisfied him and in order to have the book ready for the King's visit in August 1605, Sir Thomas had the list of donations printed up to June 1604, and the book bound in London before the end of that month. The Register has been much restored; the spine dates only from the nineteenth century, while the triangular floral ornaments are the same as those on the second volume, begun in 1693, and were probably added then. The brass clasps, corner- and centre-pieces are original; 'Anno 1604' is incised on the inner sides of the clasps. As centre- and corner-pieces from the same dies are also to be found on the Christ Church Benefactors' Register of 1614 (no. 128) and on the second volume of the Bodleian Register, bound about 1693, presumably several copies were struck and a stock kept. The enamelled arms in the centre are those of Sir Thomas Bodley, with one of the earliest uses of his motto, 'Quarta perennis'.

On: BODLEIAN LIBRARY, *Registrum donationum,* [London, R. Barker, 1604].

Folio, 415 × 325 × 105 mm. Black calf, restored late seventeenth century, rebacked nineteenth century; contemporary brass centre- and corner-pieces.

See: Sir Thomas Bodley, *Letters to Thomas James* (1926), pp. 100–3; G. G. Barber, 'Quarta perennis', *Bodleian Library Record*, VII (1962), p. 48.

Provenance: Presented by Sir Thomas Bodley, 1604.

PLATE XXVIII   BODLEIAN (Library Records)

128 AN EARLY DONORS' REGISTER   London, *c.* 1614

So far as it is known, All Souls was the first Oxford college to acquire a library donors' register (1604–05) and this was bound rather simply with the same corner-pieces as no. 120. Christ Church followed in order to record the gift of £800 from Otho Nicholson in 1613 for the restoration of the library. Nicholson, a wealthy man, who also paid for bringing a water-supply to Carfax, may have been inspired by Sir Thomas Bodley's example; certainly the same painter was employed for the ceilings of both Duke Humphrey and Christ Church (see J. C. Cole, 'The painted roof of the Old Library, Christ Church, pt. III,' *Oxoniensia*, XXVI/XXVII (1963), pp. pp. 229–31), while this register resembles that provided a decade earlier by Bodley in its use of brass centre- and corner-pieces from the same dies. Instead of metal clasps, however, there were formerly ties, for which only the slits in the leather now remain. The arms in the centre and elsewhere are those of Otho Nicholson; this stamp was also used to mark books purchased with his benefaction. The volume was rebacked in 1777, when C. M. Cracherode was Librarian, by William Hayes of Oxford at a cost of £2. 6s. 6d., including extra vellum leaves.

On: CHRIST CHURCH, Library donor's book, manuscript begun *c.* 1614.

395 × 310 × 90 mm. Brown calf, rebacked.

See: W. G. Hiscock, *A Christ Church miscellany* (1946), p. 18, n. 1 and Wake Librarian's accounts (Archives lv. b. 8).

Provenance: Acquired *c.* 1614.

CHRIST CHURCH

129 ETON CENTRE- AND CORNER-PIECE BINDING BY
WILLIAMSON   Eton, *c.* 1603

Between 1602 and 1621, while Sir Henry Savile was Provost, a
binder surnamed Williamson, of intemperate habits, was employed
by Eton College, and certain distinctive tools such as the centre- and
corner-pieces on the volume displayed enable his work to be identified. The badge of a crowned falcon holding a sceptre was used by
Elizabeth I, but this tool was apparently owned by Williamson and
does not indicate royal ownership. He was the first English binder
to tool the title of a book on the spine; no such example is known in
Oxford, but he certainly lettered the covers of the set of the Eton
Chrysostom at Trinity College with the donor's and college's names,
and the date 1612. Seven other bindings by Williamson are extant
in Oxford college libraries: another set of the Eton Chrysostom,
dated 1612, at Brasenose; Martial's *Epigrammaton* (1624) and
Herodian (1581), both with the falcon badge, and a manuscript
history of the Charterhouse (1619) at Christ Church; a fine copy of
Ben Jonson's *Workes* (1616) with painted fore-edge at Oriel; Knolles'
Historie of the Turkes (1603) at Lincoln; and a Philippe de Mornay
(1604) at St. John's.

On: J. CHAMBER, A confutation of astrologicall daemonology,
     manuscript written *c.* 1604.
     308 × 205 × 41 mm. Light brown calf, original decorated back.
See: Brassington, plate XIX; Hobson, *Cambridge,* 104–6; Nixon,
     Broxbourne, 100, 114–16; Sir R. Birley, 'The history of Eton
     College Library', *The Library,* 5th series, XI (1956), 246–9 and
     plate 6.
Provenance: Sir Henry Savile; given by him for the use of the Savilian
     professors, 1620.

PLATE XXIX   BODLEIAN (MS. Savile 42)

130 BOUND FOR HENRY, PRINCE OF WALES
                                              London, *c.* 1610

A large portion of the library built up for Prince Henry, the eldest
son of James I, who had matriculated at Magdalen in 1605, was
rebound about 1610 and the volume displayed is a typical example
of a style adopted for folios. More than one binder was probably
employed, while the tools used seem to have been shared. Three

73

variants of the Prince's armorial stamp are known, all usually with the label in silver (see no. 142). The corner ornaments of lions rampant would have had to be blocked in a press, not stamped by hand, on account of their size. After Prince Henry's untimely death in 1612 at the age of eighteen, his books passed into the Royal Library, many eventually going to the British Museum in 1757, though many others, like this volume, never reached that destination.

On: J. CUIACIUS, *Operum tomus III*, Lugduni, sumptibus Ioannis Pillehotte, 1606.
Folio, 372 × 235 × 95 mm. Brown calf, rebacked.
See: Hobson, *English*, no. 17; Nixon, *Twelve*, pp. 3–5, 10–12; Baltimore, no. 406.
Provenance: Henry, Prince of Wales; in the College in the nineteenth century.

QUEEN'S COLLEGE

131 BOUND FOR PRESENTATION TO SIR CHRISTOPHER HATTON London, *c.* 1612

This finely decorated book is one of a set of five parts printed on large paper and specially bound for the dedicatee, Sir Christopher Hatton, cousin of the Lord Chancellor of the same name, whose crest is in the centre. The corner-pieces are of an extremely common type, based on continental models as usual, and several variants are recorded although none is exactly like this.

On: O. GIBBONS, *The first set of madrigals and mottets: tenor*, London, Thomas Snodham, the assign of W. Barley, 1612.
4°, 280 × 200 × 10 mm. Dark brown calf.
See: W. G. Hiscock, *A Christ Church miscellany* (1946), p. 23.
Provenance: Sir Christopher Hatton (d. 1619); Henry Aldrich; bequeathed by him, 1710.

PLATE XXX CHRIST CHURCH

132 A LONDON BINDING London, *c.* 1600

The centre- and corner-pieces on the small volumes shown also belong to a common type of which several versions are recorded, and were used in London from about 1570 to 1640 (see Hobson, *Cambridge*, p. 102 and plate XXXVIII). The particular corner-pieces here were also used by a binder who did work for Archbishop Parker and for the Royal Library.

On: Bible in Latin, manuscript, thirteenth century.
  151 × 100 × 54 mm. Brown calf, original back.
Provenance: Sir Thomas Tresham (d. 1605), 1600; Sir Arthur Throckmorton; presented by him, 1626.

MAGDALEN COLLEGE (MS. Lat. 1)

133 POSSIBLY BOUND BY A FRENCH REFUGEE
London? *c.* 1616

The central oval wreath of foliage, with the open-work corner-pieces, suggests French workmanship, but the English printed fragments in the binding point to this country. Since the book is a presentation copy from the translator, Pierre Delaune, minister of the Walloon Church at Norwich from 1601 to 1656, to William Laud when Bishop of London, it may possibly have been the work of a member of that congregation. It is known that at least one man worked as a binder when he first came to Norwich in 1567, and he and possibly others may have brought their tools with them (see W. J. C. Moens, 'The Walloons and their church at Norwich, 1565–1832', *Publications of the Huguenot Society of London,* I (1887–88), pp. 71, 230–1). The book, however, may equally well have been bound in London, where it was printed, possibly by someone with Huguenot connections. This copy was probably given to Laud in 1628 when Delaune unsuccessfully petitioned the King for the Rectory of Stanford Rivers 'for recompence for translating the English Liturgie'.

On: La liturgie angloise, ou, Le livre des prières publiques, Londres, Iean Bill, 1616.
  4°, 214 × 155 × 40 mm. Dark brown calf, original back.
Provenance: Archbishop Laud; Brooke bequest (1911).

KEBLE COLLEGE

134 BOUND BY A BINDER WHO WORKED FOR NORTON AND BILL
London, *c.* 1617

The corner-pieces on this early seventeenth-century binding stylistically resemble those used by Williamson on no. 129, but there are several variants. The ones used here are, however, associated with a group of tools decorating other books printed by John Bill, like the volume displayed. One Richard Taylor, who worked in London from about 1601 to 1629, is named in a court case of 1616 as binding for Bill and his partners, Bonham and John Norton, and so the books with these tools may have been bound by him (see Hobson, *English*, no. 21).

On: R. MOCKET, *Doctrina et politia ecclesiae Anglicanae*, Londini, apud Ioannem Billium, 1617.
    4°, 225 × 165 × 30 mm. Dark brown calf, original spine.
Provenance: Unknown; in the College in the eighteenth century.

UNIVERSITY COLLEGE

ENGLISH BINDING IN THE REIGNS OF
JAMES I AND CHARLES I

English binding styles remained much the same between the late Elizabethan period and the Civil War although there was a tendency for
the blocks to become less heavy. This case shows bindings produced during
the latter years of the reign of James I and that of Charles I up to 1640.
The centre- and corner-piece pattern, with or without a field of small
tools, continued to be widely used, while more individuals added their
armorial bearings to the covers. Some noblemen's bindings are displayed,
together with a group of books either from the Royal Library or presentation copies to royalty, mainly acquired by Sir William Clarke when
assistant secretary to the Army Council, and now in Worcester College
(see Nixon, *Twelve*, p. 5). During the first half of the century limp vellum
grew in popularity, especially for smaller books, although it is also found
on folios, as nos. 135 and 137. A number of presentation copies in the
Royal Library were bound in this way. A study of the tools shows that
nos. 141, 143–6 and 148 came from the same shop. Sixteen bindings can
be assigned to this craftsman, all on books printed between 1624 and
1640 with the exceptions of a Bodleian copy of the Oxford verses, *Pietas
erga Jacobum* (1603) and the Royal Library copy of J. Hall's *Polemices*
(1611) now in Worcester College. It is possible these two earlier books
were bound at a later date, but no evidence is forthcoming.

135 BOUND FOR FRANCIS BACON, BARON VERULAM
England, *c.* 1619

Books with Bacon's crest on the covers are not common but several
others are known bound in limp vellum as the example shown (see
no. 170 and University of London, *Historical and armorial bookbindings
exhibited in the University Library* (1937), nos. 6–7). The overall design
of floral tools anticipates those used in England after the Restoration, especially the daisy-like flowers in the inner border.

On: G. LASSO DE LA VEGA, *Primera parte de los commentarios reales*,
Lisboa, Pedro Crasbeeck, 1619.
Folio, 264 × 185 × 30 mm. Limp vellum, original back.

See: Gibson, nos. 24, 25.
Provenance: Francis Bacon, 1st Baron Verulam (1561–1626); J. Selden (1659).

PLATE XXXI   BODLEIAN (4° V 2 Art. Seld.)

136 BOUND FOR GEORGE VILLIERS WHEN MARQUESS OF BUCKINGHAM   London? *c.* 1620

The heraldic decoration on this elaborate centre- and corner-piece binding indicates a member of the Villiers family who was a marquess. This could only be George Villiers, the court favourite, who was Marquess of Buckingham from 1618 until raised to a dukedom in 1623. The crudity of the heraldry here suggests that the binding was a gift from some seeker after his patronage rather than one commissioned by himself, especially since he used a stamp with a complete achievement when a marquess. The scallops on the shield were added separately and did not form part of the armorial block; the use of the same scallop tool in the borders further emphasizes the ownership. At some time the centre of the armorial cartouche has been cut out and relaid, but since the volume bears evidence of extensive repairs on at least two occasions, it cannot be determined whether the Villiers arms were substituted for another's, in the manner of Elkanah Settle later in the century, or whether these cuts were made when the binding was repaired.

On: R. HOLINSHED, *The chronicles of England. Newlie amended*, [London, at the expenses of J. Harison, G. Bishop, R. Newberie, H. Denham and T. Woodcocke, 1587].
Folio, 375 × 240 × 110 mm. Brown calf, rebacked with eighteenth-century spine laid on.
Provenance: George Villiers (1592–1628) when Marquess of Buckingham, 1618–23; Basil Feilding, 4th Earl of Denbigh (1668–1717).

ST. HUGH'S COLLEGE

137 BOUND FOR GEORGE VILLIERS, DUKE OF BUCKINGHAM   London, *c.* 1625

The delicately cut armorial block should be compared with the rather crude heraldry on no. 136. The coronet again indicates a marquess but Buckingham continued to use this block after he became a duke, as can be seen on a copy of R. Crakanthorp's and J. Barkham's *Defensio* of 1625 at Queen's College. As on the binding for Francis Bacon (no. 135), an overall pattern is adopted, a practice confined to limp vellum covers at this period in England. A similar pattern, but with different small tools and a larger armorial block, is used on a copy of T. Gainsford, *The glory of England* (1618), at All Souls.

On: JAMES I, *Workes*, London, Robert Barker & John Bill, 1616.
Folio, 340 × 221 × 45 mm. Limp white vellum, recased.
See: C. J. Fordyce and T. M. Knox, 'The Library of Jesus College, Oxford', *Oxford Bibliographical Society, Proceedings and papers*, V (1940), p. 63.
Provenance: George Villiers (1592–1628), Duke of Buckingham; Francis Mansell (1579–1665); presented by him, 1661.

PLATE XXXII   JESUS COLLEGE

138 POSSIBLY BOUND FOR JAMES I   London, *c.* 1620

Although the royal arms were frequently added to bindings by booksellers, there is reason to believe that this detached cover may have had a closer connection with a monarch. This particular royal block has previously been recorded on eight other books which can be associated with the Royal Library and was used up to 1634. The same block and corner-pieces are also on a Prayer Book of 1615 at St. John's College, presented by Sir William Paddy, the King's physician, in 1634. According to G. D. Hobson (*Cambridge*, p. 108), the same binder used this royal stamp and the corner-pieces on no. 139.

On: Detached book cover.
346 × 210 mm. Brown calf.
See: Brassington, plate XXI; C. Davenport, *Royal English bookbindings* (1896), p. 57 (plate V).
Provenance: James I; F. Douce (1834).

BODLEIAN (Douce Bindings A 37)

139 A LONDON BINDING WITH THE ROYAL ARMS
London, *c.* 1627

The fine *semés* of thistles and fleurs-de-lys, together with the royal arms, suggest that this volume may once have been owned by Charles

79

I, but there is no definite evidence of any connection. The armorial stamp is not recorded elsewhere. The distinctive angled corner-pieces with cherubs' heads are also on a copy of Speed's *Theatre* (1611) in Trinity College, Cambridge, used with the arms of Anne of Denmark, consort of James I. The same outer border, thistle and fleurs-de-lys can similarly be seen on no. 150, so the volume displayed can be ascribed to the same shop as this and no. 138.

On: J. SCHILLER, *Coelum stellatum Christianum*, Augustae Vindelicorum, praelo Andreae Apergeri, 1627.
Oblong folio, 321 × 390 × 30 mm. Dark brown calf, original back.
See: Hobson, *Cambridge*, plates XXXIX–XL.
Provenance: Archbishop Laud; presented by him, 1634.

PLATE XXXIII   ST. JOHN'S COLLEGE

140 PRESENTATION   COPY   FOR   THE   DUCHESS   OF
     RICHMOND AND LENNOX   London, *c.* 1624

Captain John Smith dedicated his *Generall historie of Virginia* to Frances, widow of Ludovic Stuart, Duke of Richmond and Lennox, and this is the copy specially bound 'for his approved kynd frend', as the author wrote on the title-page. The arms of the Duchess are on the covers, surmounted by a ducal coronet. The corner-pieces are also used on a Prayer Book of 1616 bound for George Abbot, Archbishop of Canterbury, at Queen's College, and on a copy of Cluverius, *Germaniae antiquae* (1616) decorated with the English royal arms, belonging to University College.

On: J. SMITH, *The generall history of Virginia*, London, printed by I.D. and I.H. for Michael Sparkes, 1624.
Folio, 332 × 220 × 33 mm. Brown calf, recased.
Provenance: Frances, Duchess of Richmond and Lennox (d. 1639).

PLATE XXXIV   QUEEN'S COLLEGE

141 A LIMP WHITE VELLUM BINDING   London, 1625

An example of limp vellum binding with centre- and corner-piece design on an ermine field is shown here. The same corner-pieces, each with a sun in splendour and a dove, are also found on two other books printed in 1625 at Oxford (BFAC, plate LXXX), and on a manuscript Garter Statutes for Edward Sackville, Earl of Dorset, at Oriel College. It was, however, more likely to have been bound in London in view of its probable origin and the fact that the tools link it to nos. 143–6 and 148.

On: Thirteen almanacs for the year 1626, London, printed for the Company of Stationers, [1625].
8°, 150 × 90 × 35 mm. Limp white vellum.
Provenance: G. Clarke (1736).

WORCESTER COLLEGE

142 BOUND FOR CHARLES I WHEN PRINCE OF WALES
London, *c.* 1620

This particular stamp of the Stuart arms with a label for cadency was also used on books bound for Charles's elder brother Henry, who died in 1612 (see no. 130 and Nixon, *Twelve,* pp. 10–11; the stamp is illustrated in University of London, *Historical and armorial bookbindings exhibited in the University Library* (1937), plate 3 and [H. M. Nixon], *Royal English bookbindings in the British Museum* (1957), plate 14A). It is found on three other books in Oxford libraries, all printed in 1610: Tycho Brahe, *Astronomiae progymnasmata* and Maginus, *Ephemerides,* both at Worcester College, and Henningus Arnisaeus, *De jure majestatis,* at Queen's. The corner-pieces, each with a distinctive flaming heart, have not been found elsewhere.

On: S. NEUGEBAUERUS, *Icones et vitae principum et regum Poloniae,* Francofurti ad Moenum, in bibliopoli Lucae Iennis, typis Hartm. Paltenii, 1620.
4°, 205 × 150 × 10 mm. Limp white vellum.
Provenance: Charles I.

ST. JOHN'S COLLEGE

143 FROM THE ROYAL LIBRARY   London, *c.* 1640

This book is another of those from the Royal Library acquired by Sir William Clarke. Cherubs' heads, which make up the centre-piece here, have been used at intervals as ornaments on bindings since the fifteenth century and were particularly fashionable in England in

81

the seventeenth century (Hobson, *English*, p. 48). This centre-piece, used by the binder of nos. 141, 144–6, 148, can also be seen on no. 146 and on a volume in the Broxbourne Library (Nixon, *Broxbourne*, no. 62), while the corner-pieces are on nos. 141, 144 and 148.

On: *Constitutions and canons ecclesiasticall*, London, by Robert Barker and by the assignes of John Bill, 1640.
4°, 215 × 162 × 8 mm. Limp white vellum.
Provenance: Charles I; G. Clarke (1736).

WORCESTER COLLEGE

144 BOUND FOR CHARLES II WHEN PRINCE OF WALES
London, *c*. 1636

This binding is another example of the work of the man who bound nos. 141, 143–6, 148. The corner-pieces on nos. 143–4, 148 are the same, but the centre-piece here is made up of nine impressions from a tool of the Prince of Wales's feathers. The cherub motif is again present as in nos. 143 and 146, but a larger tool has been used. This large paper copy, formerly in the Royal Library, was probably presented by the author to Charles, then only six years old, to whom the work was dedicated.

On: C. BUTLER, *The principles of musik*, London, John Haviland for the author, 1636.
4°, 214 × 160 × 15 mm. Limp white vellum.
See: C. H. Wilkinson, 'Worcester College library', *Oxford Bibliographical Society, Proceedings and papers*, I (1927), 299.
Provenance: Charles II when Prince of Wales; G. Clarke (1736).

WORCESTER COLLEGE

145 BOUND FOR QUEEN HENRIETTA MARIA
London, *c*. 1627

The central panel, filled with small roses and fleurs-de-lys, represents Henrietta Maria's French origin and English marriage. The outer border with a lively roll portraying squirrels, pheasants, hounds and other animals, was also used on two books printed at Oxford in 1625 (BFAC, plate LXXX) and so links this binding to the shop that also produced nos 141, 143–4, 146, 148. Besides a poem, this manuscript contains a portrait of the Queen, engraved and dated 1627, by Lucas Vorsterman the elder, a Fleming who worked in England 1622–30.

On: M. Leius, manuscript Latin poem addressed to Queen Henrietta Maria, *c.* 1627.

232 × 180 × 5 mm. Limp white vellum.

See: C. H. Wilkinson, 'Worcester College library', *Oxford Bibliographical Proceedings and papers,* I (1927), 299.

Provenance: Henrietta Maria; G. Clarke (1736).

Worcester College (MS. 60)

146   BOUND FOR THE EARL OF BRIDGEWATER
London, c. 1624

The author, Henry Mason, presented this copy to John Egerton, the 1st Earl of Bridgewater. The centre-piece with cherubs is also found on no. 143, and the triangular ornament appears on no. 144, thus linking the binding to the same shop that produced nos. 141, 143–5, 148. The spine was originally lettered with the title and author's name in ink, but at an early date it was divided into six sections by fillets and a star added on top in gilt. Since this tool has not been found elsewhere on this group of bindings, the decoration on the spine was presumably added after the book reached Lord Bridgewater's library.

On: H. Mason, *The new art of lying,* London, George Purslowe for Iohn Clarke, 1624.

4°, 201 × 147 × 12 mm. Limp white vellum.

Provenance: John Egerton, 1st Earl of Bridgewater (1579–1649); John Brand (1744–1806), lot 5524 in his sale, June 1807; Edmund Malone (1741–1812); Lord Sunderlin, presented by him, 1821.

Bodleian (Malone 742)

147   A LIMP VELLUM BINDING
London, c. 1619

This small book is an example of overall decoration applied to a vellum cover; the outer border is repeated on the spine. The regular

83

layout of the small tools compares unfavourably with the achievements of English binders after the Restoration using similar motifs.

On: A. GATTI, *La caccia*, Londra, G. Billio, 1619.
   8°, 149 × 90 × 10 mm. Limp white vellum.
Provenance: Unknown; in the College in the eighteenth century.

ALL SOULS COLLEGE

148   FROM THE ROYAL LIBRARY   London, *c.* 1640

This binding is another of Sir William Clarke's acquisitions from the royal collections and belongs to the same group as nos. 141, 143–6. The corner-pieces also appear on nos. 141, 143–4, while one of the cherub tools is on no. 144 as well. The small stamp of the royal arms in the centre is used on two other vellum bindings at Worcester College with the same provenance as the book shown here. The Queen's College copy is very similarly bound with the same corner-pieces.

On: SIR T. RYVES, *Historiae navalis mediae libri tres*, Londini, apud
   Richardum Hodgkinsonne, 1640.
   12°, 175 × 112 × 24 mm. Limp white vellum.
Provenance: Charles I; G. Clarke (1736).

WORCESTER COLLEGE

84

ENGLISH BINDINGS OF THE MID-SEVENTEENTH CENTURY

During the first half of the seventeenth century, English binders gradually ceased to follow French designs so slavishly. The use of the so-called 'Lyonese' blocked centre- and corner-pieces continued and five different examples are shown (nos. 149–53), including two dating from the reign of Charles II, to illustrate how an older style persisted after the introduction of completely fresh designs by Mearne and others. The practice of making up a centre- and corner-piece pattern by combinations of small tools, mostly floral, became more widespread, giving a foretaste of what was to come after the Restoration. Examples of this type, favoured by Lord Herbert of Cherbury (nos. 154, 157, 159) and others (no. 160) are shown, which maintain the essentials of the original oriental design. Outside London, Cambridge binders reached high standards (nos. 156, 161), while a putative Irish binding is included as well (no. 155). Morocco, or 'Turkey leather', rarely used in the sixteenth century, increased in popularity as a material for fine bindings and it is noticeable that only three in this case are in calf.

149 A CENTRE- AND CORNER-PIECE BINDING

London? *c.* 1640

This detached cover is a typical example of the so-called Lyonese centre- and corner-piece type that became popular in England during the second half of the sixteenth century. A distinctive detail is the butterfly resting in the midst of the foliage of each piece. Although the tools used here are different from those on nos. 150–3, the small and large stars filling the background are identical with those found on the binding of a manuscript of 1622, Medulla Parlamentalis, bound for Edward Gwynn (d. *c.* 1645), a barrister book-collector (see B. Quaritch Ltd., catal. 436 (1930), no. 1166). The identity of the owner of the initials 'T.S.' seen on this cover has not been established. The later inscription in the top right corner includes '1646', which may refer to the date of publication or purchase by another owner.

On: Detached book cover.
326 × 207 mm. Brown calf.
Provenance: T.S.; F. Douce (1834).

BODLEIAN (Douce Bindings A 27)

150 A LONDON BINDING WITH THE ROYAL ARMS
London, *c.* 1635

Similarly patterned, though actually different, corner-pieces from
those on nos. 149, 151–3 are used on the volume shown, but here they
are within a border enclosing the royal arms on a field of small
thistles and fleurs-de-lys. The border and small tools are identical
with those on no. 139, which has another version of the royal arms.
Numerous varieties of this type of royal stamp, with a lion's head on
each side of the cartouche, can be seen on English seventeenth-century
bindings, such as the very similar one on no. 153, and their presence
does not necessarily imply royal ownership. The armorial stamp and
corner-pieces on this volume are also used on a Prayer Book and
Psalms (1636–38) at Lady Margaret Hall. Similar arms, corner-
pieces and small tools also can be seen on a copy of Raderus, *Bavaria
pia* (1628) in the British Museum ([H. M. Nixon], *Royal English bookbindings in the British Museum* (1957), plate 8). Perhaps significantly,
this particular royal stamp is found on at least seven copies of John
Minsheu's *Ductor in linguas* (1617), all in contemporary calf. Since
'to be sold at John Brownes Shoppe, *a bookebinder in* Little Brittaine
in London' appears in the imprint, it is possible that Browne owned the
tool and was the binder. But of the two men of this name working
in London about this time, one died in 1622 and the other in 1628,
before the book displayed was published. The stamp re-appeared
after the Restoration and is found in Oxford libraries on eight of the
numerous works of William Prynne, published between 1660 and
1666 (cf. no. 153).

On: CHALCONDYLAS, *Histoire de la décadence de l'empire grec*, Paris, chez
Pierre Baillet, 1632.
Folio, 375 × 235 × 85 mm. Black morocco, original back.
Provenance: John Gennadius sale, Sotheby's, 28 Mar. 1895, lot 758.

PLATE XXXV   ASTOR DEPOSIT (C5)

151 A CENTRE- AND CORNER-PIECE BINDING
London? 1600–40

The tools used on the binding shown here are again different from those used on nos. 149–50, 152, although so similar in design. The edges of the boards are decorated with a roll of small gilt diamonds, a fashion popular with London binders between about 1600 and 1640.

On: Prophetiae Isaiae [Hebrew], Parisiis, ex officina Roberti Stephani, 1539.
4°, 247 × 168 × 51 mm. Brown calf, original spine.
Provenance: Unknown; in the College before 1860.

MAGDALEN COLLEGE

152 A CENTRE- AND CORNER-PIECE BINDING
Edinburgh? *c.* 1661

The distinctive centre- and corner-piece tools, with a butterfly resting amidst foliage, seen on nos. 149–51, were used again after the Restoration, as on the book shown here and no. 153. The outer border, decorated with a roll of dots in semi-circles, is typical of the later seventeenth century. The book itself was printed in Edinburgh by an Englishman; in the absence of any other evidence, it is difficult to determine whether it was bound in Scotland or England. As this style of binding was going out of fashion in London at this time, perhaps the new designs and tools had not yet travelled north, and the balance is probably in favour of Edinburgh.

On: SIR A. PRIMEROSE, *Laws and acts of the first Parliament of Charles II holden at Edinburgh, 1661*, Edinburgh, Evan Tyler, 1661.
4°, 278 × 185 × 18 mm. Black morocco, original back.
Provenance: Possibly part of the bequest of George Clarke (1736).

WORCESTER COLLEGE

153 A CORNER-PIECE BINDING WITH THE ROYAL ARMS
London? *c.* 1668

As no. 152, this binding is another example of the post-Restoration use of corner-piece tools showing a butterfly amid foliage, popular before the Civil Wars. The rolls used in the borders are typically late seventeenth-century English specimens (see also nos. 219–21, 226, 233). This particular stamp of the royal arms has not been found elsewhere; however, other works written by William Prynne (1600–69) are known with the stamp used on no. 150. Prynne became Keeper of the Records in the Tower after the Restoration, which may account for the presence of these arms. Contemporaries thought his manners old-fashioned, and maybe his choice of bindings for presentation copies similarly echoed an earlier period.

On: W. PRYNNE, *An additional appendix to Aurum Reginae*, London, printed for the author by Tho. Ratcliffe and Th. Daniel, and are to be sold by Edward Thomas and Josias Robinson, 1668. 4°, 243 × 180 × 12 mm. Red morocco, original back.
Provenance: John Brand (1744–1806).

ASTOR DEPOSIT (C7)

154 BOUND FOR LORD HERBERT OF CHERBURY
London, *c.* 1638

The style of this binding is reminiscent of that used by Cambridge craftsmen but it seems probable that Lord Herbert patronized London shops. Combinations of small tools returned to fashion in the early years of the seventeenth century in England, though blocked centre- and corner-pieces continued to be popular. The consequent superior results of massing these smaller tools in the corners and centres are evident on the example displayed. The tools are different from those on nos. 157 and 159, also bound for Lord Herbert. Of the two mottoes found on bindings for Lord Herbert, the earlier is seen here; the other one is on no. 159. Besides this manuscript, others bound in blue morocco with similar tools came from the same benefactor. It is interesting that Archbishop Juxon, much of whose library is now in St. John's College, favoured a similar style on books bound for him in the 1630s (see no. 160).

On: EDWARD, LORD HERBERT OF CHERBURY, Life and raigne of King Henry the VIII, manuscript, 1638.
350 × 222 × 85 mm. Dark blue calf, original back.
See: Philip, plate 17; *Book Collector*, XIV (1965), p. 60.
Provenance: Presented by the author, 1644.

BODLEIAN (MS. Bodley 910)

155 A POSSIBLE IRISH BINDING WITH THE ROYAL ARMS
Dublin? *c.* 1640

The layout of the small tools and the general style of binding resemble those in vogue in England in the 1630s, but in view of the imprint and authorship of the book displayed it is possible it was bound in Ireland. The border roll with three small circles alternating with an oblong is designed similarly to, though actually different from, that used on no. 160, for instance. The Dublin Company of Stationers was closely allied to its London counterpart which, about 1617, established booksellers and binders in Dublin 'to furnish the Kingdom plentifully with whatever they shall want' (British Museum, Sloane MS. 4756, f. 153, quoted by R. Munter, *The history of the Irish newspaper* (1967), p. 3). This particular block of the royal arms also appears on both the Merton and Exeter College copies of Thomas Milles's *Catalogue of honor*, printed in London in 1610, so it may have been one of the tools sent across to Ireland. However, the fact that no other gilt bindings seem to have been produced in Dublin in the remaining sixty years of the seventeenth century may argue against the Irish thesis.

On: J. Ussher, Archbishop of Armagh, *Britannicarum ecclesiarum antiquitates*, Dublinii, ex officina typographica Societatis Bibliopolarum, 1640.
4°, 195 × 135 × 75 mm. Dark blue morocco, original back.
See: C. H. Wilkinson, 'Worcester College library', *Oxford Bibliographical Society, Proceedings and papers*, I (1927), p. 298.
Provenance: Charles I?; G. Clarke (1736).

PLATE XXXVI   WORCESTER COLLEGE

156 A CAMBRIDGE BINDING, PERHAPS BY JOHN HOULDEN
Cambridge, *c.* 1643

The book shown here was given by Henry Rich, 1st Earl of Holland, to whom it was dedicated as Chancellor of Cambridge University, to John Selden. As it was printed in Cambridge, this copy was presumably one of those specially bound for presentation purposes and at this time John Houlden received these special commissions (J. C. T. Oates, 'Cambridge books of congratulatory verses, 1603–1640, and their binders', *Transactions of the Cambridge Bibliographical Society*, I (1953), pp. 410–11). There is a very similar binding on

89

another copy of this book in Cambridge University Library. Some of the tools used here are also found on other books with Cambridge connections now ascribed to John Houlden (see *Book Collector*, VII (1958), p. 396; Nixon, *Broxbourne*, 144–6). One of the most distinctive features is the arrangement of ellipses and small circles between the upper and lower ends of the central lozenge and the inner border, which can also be seen on no. 161.

On: BEDE, *Historiae ecclesiae gentis anglorum libri V*, Cantabrigiae, Rogerus Daniel, 1643.
Folio, 353 × 230 × 40 mm. Black morocco, original back with contemporary lettering.
Provenance: Henry Rich, 1st Earl of Holland (1590–1649); J. Selden (1659).

PLATE XXXVII   BODLEIAN (S. Seld. c.21)

157 BOUND BY THE HERBERT OF CHERBURY BINDER
London? *c.* 1633

Edward, Lord Herbert of Cherbury, implies in his autobiography (*The autobiography of Edward, Lord Herbert of Cherbury*, with introduction, notes, by S. Lee, 2nd ed. [1907], p. 134) that most of the copies of his *De veritate* were given away to friends and scholars. At least six copies are known bound in red morocco similar to the one shown here, including the unpublished example at St. John's College with less elaborate tooling. Only one has the sheaf of arrows crest, usually found on the Latin edition of 1639 (no. 159). The pattern is made up from numerous small tools, filling the covers more densely than in work by Lord Herbert's other binder (no. 154). The general style bears some resemblance to French binding of the period, but it is thought that Lord Herbert is more likely to have employed a London craftsman.

On: EDWARD, LORD HERBERT OF CHERBURY, *De veritate*, Londini, per Augustinum Matthaeum, 1633.
4°, 233 × 174 × 33 mm. Red morocco, original back.
See: Philip, plate 16; *Book Collector*, XIV (1965), p. 60.
Provenance: Presented by the author, 1633.

BODLEIAN (4° X 63 Jur.)

158 BOUND FOR CHARLES II WHEN PRINCE OF WALES
London? *c.* 1638

The background of small roses and dots with the proportionately overlarge centre-piece continues a style, begun in Elizabeth's reign, of overloading covers with gilt, but here the floral borders and corner-pieces of foliage lighten the overall impression somewhat. The stamp of the Prince of Wales's feathers had formerly been used on books bound for both sons of James I: Henry Frederick (C. Davenport, *Royal English bookbindings* (1896), pp. 60–61) and Charles I (on a Tasso in Worcester College). The author, a royal chaplain, had dedicated the first edition of this book to Charles I, but changed to Charles II, then only eight years old, for the second.

On: A. Ross, *Virgilii evangelisantis Christiados libri XIII*, Londini, J. Legate for R. Thrale, 1638.
    8°, 142 × 96 × 30 mm. Dark blue morocco, original back.
See: C. H. Wilkinson, 'Worcester College library', *Oxford Bibliographical Society, Proceedings and papers*, I (1927), p. 319 and plate facing p. 298.
Provenance: Charles II; G. Clarke (1736).

WORCESTER COLLEGE

159 BOUND BY THE HERBERT OF CHERBURY BINDER
London? *c.* 1639

Several presentation copies are known of the French translation of Lord Herbert of Cherbury's *De veritate* which, like the original version, are all similarly bound and decorated with the same tools used in 1633 (no. 157). Eight of the nine recorded copies have the author's crest of a sheaf of arrows with the motto ΕΥΣΤΟΧΩΣ, which he seems to have substituted about this time for ΑΠΛΑΝΩΣ (see no. 154). The profusion of small tools is less exuberant, and with a more pleasing result, than the binding on the presentation copies of the Latin editions (no. 157).

On: EDWARD, LORD HERBERT OF CHERBURY, *De la verité*, 3e éd., [Paris], 1639.
    4°, 230 × 160 × 27 mm. Red morocco, original back.
See: *Book Collector*, XIV (1965), p. 60.
Provenance: Edward, 1st Earl of Gainsborough (1640–89); John Fitzwilliam; bequeathed by him, 1699.

MAGDALEN COLLEGE

160 AN ENGLISH BINDING DECORATED WITH SMALL
TOOLS London? *c.* 1630

The style of this binding with a central lozenge and corner-pieces
made up of small tools, mainly volutes and flowers, bears a strong
resemblance to the books bound for Lord Herbert of Cherbury
(nos. 154, 157, 159) and by Cambridge craftsmen (no. 156), but no
tools are shared with either group. A copy of Patrick Young's
edition of *Catena Graecorum patrum in Iob* (1637), formerly owned by
Archbishop Juxon and now in St. John's College, is bound with a
similar design using some of the tools used on the book displayed.

On: A. SCOTO, *Itinerario, overo nova descrittione de' viaggi principali
d'Italia*, Padoa, Francesco Bolzetta, 1629.
8°, 158 × 101 × 54 mm. Blue morocco, original back.
Provenance: Unknown; in the College before 1871.

BALLIOL COLLEGE

161 A CAMBRIDGE BINDING BY JOHN HOULDEN
Cambridge, 1662

The very distinctive pattern of a series of parallelograms one inside
the other with a central onlay is recorded on nine other books
printed between 1634 and 1662, whose bindings can be ascribed to
Cambridge (Hobson, *Cambridge*, p. 118). John Houlden, who probably bound no. 156, was almost certainly the craftsman responsible
for the book displayed since there is documentary evidence that he
bound copies of these verses for the University (J. C. T. Oates,
'Cambridge books of congratulatory verses, 1603–1640, and their
binders', *Transactions of the Cambridge Bibliographical Society*, I (1953),
p. 411). The doublure of the copy of *Basilika, the workes of King
Charles the Martyr* (1662) formerly owned by Major J. R. Abbey
(Hobson, *English*, plate 46A; J. R. Abbey sale, lot 187) has a design
practically the same as on the work shown here, and the same tools are
used in the same positions. The pattern of ellipses and small circles
in the centre can also be seen on no. 156 and on a copy of Sir Francis
Vere's *Commentaries* (1657) in the Broxbourne Library (Nixon,
Broxbourne, pp. 144–6).

On: CAMBRIDGE UNIVERSITY, *Epithalamia Cantabrigiensia in nuptias Caroli II*, Cantabrigiae, ex officina Joannis Field, 1662.
4°, 210 × 160 × 12 mm. Black morocco, original back.
Provenance: Unknown; in the College in the early nineteenth century.

PLATE XXXVIII   ST. JOHN'S COLLEGE.

ENGLISH TEXTILE AND EMBROIDERED BINDINGS

Velvet bindings, often completely plain, were popular in the early sixteenth century on the Continent but because of the weakness of the material few have survived. Some embroidered bindings followed (see no. 27) but in general there were, both then and in the seventeenth century, far fewer than in England. Queen Elizabeth had all the books in her library bound in velvet and is herself traditionally credited with some embroidered specimens (see no. 162). She was certainly presented with others (no. 163), but the main period of production was the 1620s and 1630s. Much of this work was professional and a petition submitted to Archbishop Laud in 1638 by the milliners of the Royal Exchange makes claims on behalf of the 'Imbroderers working in their own homes' who had for many years covered Bibles, Testaments and Psalm books for the 'nobility and gentry' (see Bodleian Library, MS. Tanner 67, fol. 33). It has not, however, been possible to identify the work of individual professional binders or embroiderers although the names of one or two amateurs have survived. Velvet was used again in the nineteenth century but embroidered work was rare, although the latest fine binding in this style in Oxford dates from 1906 (Trinity College: on H. C. Moffat, *Old Oxford plate*).

162 POSSIBLY BOUND BY QUEEN ELIZABETH

Ashridge, 1544

A translation from the French of 'The Miroir or glasse of the synnefull soule', a New Year's gift from Queen Elizabeth, when eleven years old, to her step-mother Queen Katherine Parr, made by her and written in her own hand. The binding with its initials KP is also said traditionally to be her work. A similar New Year's present for 1546 is in the British Museum.

On: The Miroir or glasse of the synnefull soule, manuscript written at Ashridge, 1544.
      185 × 135 × 30 mm. Silver purl in plaited braid stitch on blue silk couched ground.

94

See: T. Hearne, *Remarks and Collections,* II, (Oxford Hist. Soc. VII, 1886), pp. 131–2; C. Davenport, *English embroidered bookbindings* (1899), plate 4; Brassington, p. 28; Bodleian postcard 22; J. E. Neale, *Queen Elizabeth* (1934), p. 23.
Provenance: Francis Cherry (1729).

BODLEIAN (MS. Cherry 36)

163 PRESENTED TO QUEEN ELIZABETH   London, 1583

Described as 'one of the most decorative and in many ways the finest of all the remaining embroidered books of the time', this Bible was presented to the Queen by the printer on New Year's day 1584. He received 11¼ ounces of gilt plate for his gift which was described as 'couered wt crymson vellat alouer embradered wythe venys golde and seade perle' (British Museum, Egerton MS. 3052). In 1953 this pattern was used by James Templeton & Co. for a 'Tudor Rose' Wilton carpet design (see *The Cabinet Maker,* 19 Dec. 1953). A section of this carpet is shown by the courtesy of the manufacturers.

On: The Bible, London, Christopher Barker, 1583.
    Folio, 427 × 287 × 110 mm. Gold, silver and coloured silks on crimson velvet. Fore-edge gilt and gauffered.
See: Davenport, pp. 67–69, plate 25; Brassington, plate XVIII; A. F. Kendrick, *English decorative fabrics* (1934), plate 5; Worshipful Company of Goldsmiths *and* Oxford Society, *Treasures of Oxford* (1953), no. 197 and plate XXXIX; G. W. Digby, *Elizabethan embroidery* (1963), plate 43; *Elizabethan embroidery,* (British Council exhibition, Munich, 1964), plate XXI.
Provenance: F. Douce (1834).

FRONTISPIECE   BODLEIAN (Douce Bib. Eng. 1583 b.1)

164 ROYAL EMBROIDERED BINDING   London, *c.* 1560

An inset frame of raised silverwork, similar in design to contemporary gold-tooled leatherwork, contains the cypher ER, Tudor rose and crown. Possibly formerly the property of Queen Elizabeth.

On: Biblia sacra, Parisiis, ex officina Roberti Stephani, 1545.
8°, 200 × 130 × 80 mm. Maroon velvet with silver and coloured threads.
Provenance: Gift of Richard Allestree, 18 Jan. 1680.

CHRIST CHURCH

165 EMBROIDERED BINDING   London, *c.* 1560

Though the book is French the cover is probably English since after 1535, as a result of the treaties between François I and the Ottoman empire, Turkey leather (the modern 'morocco') became fashionable in France and largely replaced embroidered bindings. The latter remained popular in England.

On: I. RINGHIERI, *Dialogue de la vie et de la mort*, Lyon, Robert Granjon, 1558.
8°, 151 × 113 × 20 mm. Red satin and silver thread.
See: Brassington, plate XIV.
Provenance: Acquired *c.* 1626.

BODLEIAN (MS. Bodl. 660)

166 A TENT STITCH BINDING   London, *c.* 1630

A tent stitch binding decorated with two birds, a cornflower, honeysuckle, daffodil and pink with, in the centre, a rose. The ground is worked in silver herringbone stitch and is characteristic of the 1630s.

On: The Book of Common Prayer and *New Testament*, London, Robert Barker, 1630, 1631, with *Book of Psalms*, London, for the Company of Stationers, 1630.
4°, 200 × 140 × 70 mm. Silver and coloured thread on canvas.
See: Brassington, plate XXII.

BODLEIAN (C.P. 1630 e.3)
This item is exhibited in the large case at the end of the exhibition.

167 A LITTLE GIDDING BINDING   Little Gidding, *c.* 1640

This Harmony, or 'Concordance' as it was then called, was made up from cut-out Bible engravings and bound by members of the

Anglican community, or free association, founded by Nicholas Ferrar and his nieces at Little Gidding, Huntingdonshire. It is, like a number of their other productions, bound in velvet and gold-tooled in a Cambridge style. Instruction in binding was given by a Cambridge binder's daughter, possibly Katharine Moody. Ferrar died in 1636 but the community remained in being for some twenty years.

On: *The whole law of God as it is delivered in the five books of Moyses,* Little Gidding, 1640.
Folio, 500 × 370 × 42 mm. Purple velvet.
See: Hobson, *Cambridge,* p. 122, list no. V.

ST. JOHN'S COLLEGE

168 EMBROIDERED MEDALLION BINDING   London, *c.* 1640

The raised silver thread medallions protect pictures, worked in coloured silks, and showing, on the upper cover, Plenty, and on the lower, Peace. The general ground is of white satin and it is decorated with animals and fruits. Several examples of this binding design are known. The sun's rays are made of small metal strips held down by cross stitches.

On: *The Book of Common Prayer* and *Bible,* London, by Robert Barker, . . . and by the assignes of John Bill, 1639, 1640.
8°, 192 × 152 × 55 mm. Silver thread and coloured silks on white satin.
See: Brassington, plate xxiii; C. Davenport, *English embroidered bookbindings* (1899), p. 92; A. F. Kendrick, *English needlework* (1967), p. 106.

PLATE XXXIX   BODLEIAN (Arch. A d.5)

169 BOUND FOR JAMES I   London, 1623

A most unusual binding, presumably for presentation to the King although the work is dedicated to the Prince of Wales. The design, which to some extent treats the two covers as one, was executed either by impressing heated blind tools on the velvet or by carefully shaving away part of the uncut velvet. It shows a crowned thistle on the upper cover and crowned rose on the lower.

97

On: AELFRIC, *A Saxon treatise concerning the Old and New Testament* [edited by W. Lisle], London, Iohn Haviland, for Henrie Seile, 1623.

4°, 197 × 150 × 20 mm. Cut and uncut velvet.

Provenance: Gift of John Pottinger *c.* 1680.

CORPUS CHRISTI COLLEGE

170 GILT VELVET PRESENTATION BINDING   London, 1620

The *Instauratio magna*, of which this second part, the *Novum Organum*, was the first published, was amongst the most important of the philosophical works of Francis Bacon (1561–1626), who was created Viscount St. Albans the year after its publication. Bacon, who was Lord Chancellor, presented this copy to the University and a similar one to Cambridge, both volumes bearing his crest (see also no. 135) on the lower cover. The form of the University motto on the arms on the upper cover, *Sapientia Felicitas*, was similar to that used by Barnes, the University printer, in the later sixteenth century and recorded by the contemporary herald Guillim as the University motto (see E. A. Greening Lamborn, 'The arms of Oxford', *Oxford*, V (1938), p. 42).

On: F. BACON, *Instauratio magna*, Londini, apud Joannem Billium, 1620.

Folio, 340 × 212 × 35 mm. Gilt tooling on purple velvet.

See: W. D. Macray, *Annals of the Bodleian Library* (1890), p. 63; Gibson, no. 25.

Provenance: Presented by the author, 1620.

BODLEIAN (Arch. A c.5)

171 ROYAL PRESENTATION BINDING   London, 1620

On 29 May 1620 this copy of King James's works, edited by Bishop Montague, was presented to the University on behalf of the King by Patrick Young, the Librarian at St. James's, at a solemn ceremony which was the occasion for a 'verie prettie speech' from Bodley's Librarian who placed the book 'in archivis . . . with a great deale of respect'. Besides much entertainment Young received £20 from the University and later reported that the King 'was exceeding well pleased with the letters from the Universitie, and with our relation of all that passed, and does preferre Oxford unto . . . Cambridge' (see *Gentleman's magazine*, 1801, p. 980). The King autographed the volume which bore a fulsome dedication written out by his secretary. This gift had, of course, been to some extent foreshadowed by the statue of the King on the Tower of the Five Orders in the Library Quadrangle which had been completed some two years previously. He is there shown giving copies of his works, on the one hand to Fame, armed with her trumpet, and on the other to the University kneeling in humble guise.

The binding may well have been provided by one of the publishers since it is noticeable that the book was, surprisingly, not produced by the King's Printer, R. Barker. Norton and Barker had previously been on very close terms but were at this time at loggerheads. The decoration is, in general, not unlike work done on other books for Barker and for John Norton, Bonham Norton's cousin, although the imposition of the gilt leather armorial stamp and corner-pieces on the velvet is unusual. The other publisher, John Bill, was also a partner in the King's Printing House and is known to have supplied books for the royal and other libraries, being referred to on occasion as 'Bill, the bookbinder' (see H. M. Nixon, 'A binding supplied by John Bill', *Book Collector*, II (1962), p. 6, and also the notes to no. 134 in this catalogue). The King presented a similar copy of his works to Cambridge University.

On: JAMES I, *Opera*, Londini, apud Bonhamum Nortonium et Iohannem Billium, 1619.
    Folio, 345 × 220 × 50 mm. Red velvet with onlays of gilt leather.
See: W. D. Macray, *Annals of the Bodleian Library* (1890), pp. 58–60.
Provenance: Presented by James I in 1620.

BODLEIAN (Arch. A b.3)

172 EMBROIDERED PRESENTATION BINDING London, 1623

This first part of the *Instauratio magna*, published three years after the second, was, like the latter (see no. 170), presented by the author. Here the light blue velvet is decorated with a border in silver thread imitating the azured tools popular with continental binders in previous decades. Though similarly based on velvet this binding contrasts in style with that on the *Novum Organum* (see no. 170) and appears to be rather old-fashioned.

On: F. Bacon, *Opera . . . Tomus primus, qui continet de dignitate &
augmentis scientiarum libros IX* [ed. by W. Rawley], Londini, in
officina Iohannis Haviland, 1623.
Folio, 335 × 225 × 36 mm. Silver thread on light blue velvet.
Provenance: Presented by the author, 1623.

Bodleian (Arch. A c.6)

173 BOUND FOR THE DUKE OF BUCKINGHAM
London, 1625

A well-documented binding on a book dedicated and presented to
George Villiers, Duke of Buckingham, whose portrait, after the
engraving by S. de Passe, is worked on both covers. He is shown
wearing an olive-yellow doublet, pleated falling collar and the
blue ribbon of the Order of the Garter. After the Duke's assassination
on 23 August 1628 it passed to L. Roberts, a London merchant, who
presented it in 1628 to the Bodleian 'as a monument for future times'.

On: F. Bacon, *Essayes*, London, Iohn Haviland for Hanna Barret,
and Richard Whitaker, 1625.
4°, 220 × 160 × 30 mm. Dark green velvet with silver thread, the
portrait worked in darning and satin stitches on white satin over
fine white canvas.
See: Brassington, p. 29; C. Davenport, *English embroidered bookbindings*
(1899), plate 31; J. L. Nevinson, 'Embroidered miniature
portraits of Charles I', *Apollo*, 1965, pp. 310–12: A. F. Kendrick, *English needlework* (1967), p. 104.
Provenance: G. Villiers; L. Roberts; presented 1628.

Bodleian (Arch. G e.36)

174 EMBROIDERED BINDING
London, *c.* 1630

Bound with a great depth of silver thread and purl, or coiled wire,
and copiously decorated with seed pearls.

On: G. Carleton, *A thankfull remembrance of God's Mercie*, 3rd ed.,
London, M. Flesher for R. Mylbourne, and H. Robinson,
1627.

8°, 200 × 150 × 35 mm. Silver thread and pearls on mauve velvet with red silk.

See: C. H. Wilkinson, 'Worcester College library', *Oxford Bibliographical Society, Proceedings and papers*, I (1927), p. 299.

WORCESTER COLLEGE

SEVENTEENTH-CENTURY CONTINENTAL BINDINGS

The number of both royal and private collectors increased greatly through the century, encouraged by such books as Gabriel Naudé's *Advis pour dresser une bibliothèque* (1627) and Louis Jacob's *Traicté des plus belles bibliothèques* (1644). Most large collectors such as Richelieu, Mazarin, or Colbert, however, took Naudé's advice, 'Il n'est point besoin de faire une dépense extraordinaire à leur reliure', and followed de Thou's example in having a plain binding decorated only with an armorial stamp.

Very fine decorative work was, however, also produced and several styles, often derived from earlier ones, are found concurrently. Italian binding in particular, although more ornate and baroque, relied largely on versions of the earlier strapwork and fanfare styles and from around 1630 developed into a fairly distinct Roman compartment style. The leading bindery was the papal, or Rospigliosi, bindery whose latest work was done for Queen Christina of Sweden about 1680. In France the century opens with the continued and predominant use of the *semé* of fleurs-de-lys or initials regularly disposed all over the cover and a spine which is still flat. By the mid-1630s, however, the bands re-appear on the spine, lace-like border rolls come into use, while the main area of the cover, still divided up into compartments in the fanfare manner, is now decorated with a series of curled volutes or other non-representational tools, all in dotted outline. This *pointillé* gives a new tone and sophistication to bindings and may be used to heighten the contrast of some of the new mosaic compartments. Italy and the Netherlands also share a particular predilection for a version of the centre and corner design using fan-like elements.

175 *SEMÉ* BINDING FOR MARIE DE MÉDICIS   Paris, 1610

Plain *semé* binding of fleurs-de-lys with the arms of France, Medici and Austria and the crowned M monogram of Marie de Médicis (1573–1642), presumably bound for her the year her husband, Henri IV, was assassinated. The publisher, Pierre Mettayer, was a frequent business partner of Clovis Eve, son of Nicolas Eve (*relieur du roi*, 1578–81) and himself *relieur du roi* from 1584 to 1634.

On: P. MATTHIEU, *Histoire de Lovys XI roy de France,* Paris, chez P. Mettayer et la veufve M. Guillemot, 1610.

Folio, 352 × 224 × 47 mm. Red morocco. Edges gilt.

Provenance: Marie de Médicis; F. Douce (1834).

BODLEIAN (Douce M subt. 5)

176 MOURNING BINDING FOR MARIE DE MÉDICIS
Paris, 1611

Black morocco binding tooled in blind in a derivative fanfare style. The magnificently illuminated dedication and decoration record that it was presented to Marie de Médicis by her treasurer Claude Maugis (died 1658), Abbot *in commendam* of St. Ambrose, Bourges. Maugis was largely instrumental in getting Rubens to decorate the Luxembourg and corresponded with him. He was also the patron of Philippe de Champaigne. In his dedication he makes much play of Justice and Piety being the two pillars upholding the state—possibly a reference to Marie's monogram as shown on this binding.

On: Officium Beatae Virginis Mariae, (Antwerpiae, ex officina Plantiniana, apud Ioannem Moretum, 1609).

4°, 233 × 170 × 50 mm. Black morocco.

Provenance: Marie de Médicis; C. Chauncy; F. Douce (1834).

BODLEIAN (Douce BB 169)

177 BOUND FOR HENRI IV
Paris, *c.* 1605

A *semé* binding with the arms of France and Navarre. The cornerpieces recall the style of the 1580s while the small floral tools are like those of the 1590s. The floral touches of the decoration are particularly apt in view of the pharmaceutical nature of the manuscript and are found on vellum bindings by Clovis Eve (see no. 175) around this date. The endpapers bear the painted arms of Henri IV and Marie de Médicis and thus presumably date the book, and binding, to between their marriage in 1599 and the King's assassination in 1610.

On: P. PLASSARD, of Lyon, Secreti eccellentissimi esperimentati da molti huomini del mundo nel quale si contiene il modo di fare olii diversi ceroti . . . et altre sorte de medicamenti, illuminated manuscript of *c.* 1605.

287 × 210 × 30 mm. Red morocco. Fore-edge gilt and gauffered.

Provenance: Henri IV.

ASTOR DEPOSIT (A21)

178 FLEUR-DE-LYS *SEMÉ* BINDING   Paris, 1612

A typical plain *semé* contemporary binding. The spine is still flat but the number of border rolls or ornaments has increased. The outer roll is of the common pattern alternating a small square with a larger circle, but the latter part has here a close resemblance to the fanfare volute. The publisher is again P. Mettayer (see no. 175).

On: J. BARCLAY, *Pietas sive publicae pro regibus et principibus vindiciae,* Parisiis, ex typis P. Mettayer, 1612.

4°, 232 × 170 × 41 mm. Red morocco.

ALL SOULS COLLEGE

179 ITALIAN BINDING FOR HENRI IV   Rome, 1609

An Italian version of the centre- and corner-piece style where those areas have been made up with typical contemporary Italian tools which include a snail also found on a Vatican Bible of 1592. This binding seems to come from the Roman bindery which also produced nos. 21 and 185. The French royal arms are also made up with separate tools.

On: F. M. DE POPOLO, *Vaticanae lucubrationes,* Romae, ex typographia Vaticana, 1609.

Folio, 417 × 280 × 64 mm. Red morocco.

Provenance: Henri IV.

PLATE XL   ALL SOULS COLLEGE

180 BOUND FOR LOUIS XIII   Paris, 1620

A *semé* of alternate fleurs-de-lys and crowned L's was a common background on royal bindings under Louis XIII (1610–43). Five out of the eight books bearing Louis XIII's arms known in Oxford have this *semé*. Among these there are at least two variants of this block of the royal arms and the crowned L is in some cases of a plainer design.

The pastedowns here (and in no. 183) are of marbled paper which was only just beginning to come into use and is first recorded in Western Europe, being imported from Turkey, in 1598.

On: PINDAR, *Olympia, Pythia* . . . *Iohannes Benedictus repurgavit,* Salmurii, ex typis Petri Piededii, 1620.
4°, 240 × 175 × 50 mm. Olive calf.
Provenance: P. Giffart.

QUEEN'S COLLEGE

181 FLEUR-DE-LYS *SEMÉ* BINDING   Paris, *c.* 1620

The *semé* is here varied by diagonal *pointillé* lines. The pattern of the outer roll, based on a square, circle, lozenge and oval, was common throughout the century.

On: Officium hebdomadae sanctae secundum Missale & Breviarium Romanum, Parisiis, apud Sebastianum Huré, 1619.
8°, 186 × 117 × 30 mm. Olive morocco.

ASTOR DEPOSIT (D9)

182 BOUND FOR RICHELIEU   Paris, *c.* 1620

A floral centre and corner design with a wide border of fleurs-de-lys *semé* offsets the arms of Armand-Jean Du Plessis, Duc de Richelieu, (1585–1642). The binding would seem to date from before 1622 when Richelieu became a cardinal. The central field is still decorated with *S fermés.*

Richelieu's library was one of the largest of his day and, based on the town library of La Rochelle, granted to him by Louis XIII after its capture in 1628, it contained many Oriental and Hebrew manuscripts as well as the Loménie historical collections in 358 volumes all bound in red morocco by Le Gascon.

On: E. DE L'AIGUE, *In omnes C. Plinii Secundi naturalis historiae libros commentaria*, Parrisiis, apud Galliotum Pratensem, 1530.
Folio, 310 × 210 × 60 mm. Light brown.
Provenance: Duc de Richelieu; Rheims chapter library; F. Douce (1834).

BODLEIAN (Douce A subt. 39)

183 BOUND FOR ANNE OF AUSTRIA Paris, 1631

A *semé* binding alternating the Queen's monogram with the fleur-de-lys, in the style popular under Louis XIII. The outer lozenge–square–circle roll is similar in design to the one on no. 181 but of a larger size. Jean Gombauld, the author (1570–1666), frequented the Hôtel de Rambouillet and was a founder member of the Académie Française, founded in 1634. In an earlier work, *Endymion* (1624), he had, under a transparent allegory, expressed his love for the Queen Mother, Marie de Médicis, to whom this work is dedicated. The pastedowns of this book are marbled (see no. 180).

On: J. O. DE GOMBAULD, *L'Amaranthe, pastorale*, Paris, chez François Pomeray, Anthoine de Sommaville et André Soubron, 1631.
8°, 176 × 116 × 15 mm. Olive-green morocco.
See: C. H. Wilkinson, 'Worcester College library', *Oxford Bibliographical Society, Proceedings and papers*, I (1927), pp. 319–20 and plate facing p. 300; Worshipful Company of Goldsmiths *and* Oxford Society, *Treasures of Oxford* (1953), no. 205.
Provenance: G. Clarke (1736).

WORCESTER COLLEGE

184 TRANSITIONAL BAROQUE BINDING Padua? *c.* 1600

A curvilinear strapwork binding with open and baroque tools of a style popular in northern Italy around 1600 (see P. Colombo, *La legatura artistica* (1952), ch. 15). This book comes from the same workshop as the dedication copy of another book with Paduan connections bound for Cardinal Montelparo in 1594.

On: F. Piccolomini, *In academia Patavina philosophi primi*, Venetiis, apud Francescum de Franciscis, 1596.
Folio, 330 × 224 × 30 mm. Red morocco. Formerly four ties.
See: BFAC, no. P29.
Provenance: T. R. Buchanan (1941).

PLATE XLI   BODLEIAN (Buchanan c.15)

185 PAPAL EDITION   Rome, 1610

This relatively plain binding seems to have some tools in common with those on books bound for Clement VIII (1592–1605) and may come from a papal bindery since it covers a work supported by Paul V (1605–21), who took a keen interest in the printing of Arabic and acquired for the Vatican the library of Cardinal Pole (see also nos. 21 and 179).

On: 'Abd al-Wahhâb ibn Ibrâhîm al-Zanjânî, *Liber Tasriphi,* [Rome], ex typographia Medicaea linguarum externarum, 1610.
4°, 271 × 194 × 20 mm. Red morocco. Four ties.

BODLEIAN (EE 20 Art. Seld.)

186 GRIMALDI PRESENTATION BINDING   Monaco? 1620

The large armorial stamp on this presentation binding bears the arms of Honoré II Grimaldi impaling those of Trivulzio, for his wife Hippolyta. Honoré II later overthrew Spanish control and put himself under the protection of Louis XIII.

On: G. F. Monno, Portolano della maggior parte de luoghi da stantiar navi et galee in tutto il mare meditrraneo [*sic*], manuscript written in Monaco, 1620.
298 × 222 × 20 mm. Red morocco. Rebacked.
Provenance: W. J. Moore Brabazon 1848.

TAYLOR INSTITUTION

187 BOUND FOR CARDINAL BARBERINI   Rome? 1633

A relatively plain binding but still exemplifying the large central oval often found on Italian bindings of this period. The arms are those of Antonio Barberini (1608–71), created cardinal in 1628 by his relative Urban VIII (1623–44) in the heyday of Barberini power.

On: B. GATTI, *Maria regina di Scotia, poema heroico,* (Bologna), N. Tebaldini, 1633.
4°, 237 × 167 × 33 mm. Red morocco.

WORCESTER COLLEGE

188 BINDING WITH PENDANT CRESCENTS   Rome? *c.* 1610

A binding which in general style, in the use of a series of pendant crescents, and, possibly, by the use of certain tools, resembles one made for Aloysius Conticelli (see I. Schunke, 'Drei italienische Einbände des 17. Jahrhunderts', *Gutenberg Jahrbuch*, 1958, pp. 330–4). One of the associated bindings bears the arms of Clement VIII (1592–1605) but another, rather closer to the present binding in style, is dated 1617.

On: V. CARTARI, *Le imagini de i dei de gli antichi,* Venetia, Francesco Ziletti, 1580.
4°, 222 × 152 × 36 mm. Red morocco. Edges gilt and gauffered. Rebacked and repaired.
Provenance: G. Libri sale, 25 July 1862, no. 116; W. Ridler catal. Sept. 1892, no. 87; T. R. Buchanan (1941).

BODLEIAN (Buchanan e.7)

189 A VARIOUSLY BOUND SET   Naples? 1603–14

This surprising set, presumably bound as each volume appeared, evidently all comes from the same binder and shows a wide range of contemporary tool designs. This may also be the workshop which produced a diploma binding for G. F. Rossi di Gallicchio (see P. Colombo, *La legatura artistica* (1952), fig. 142). Noticeable among the tools, besides the usual crowns, flowers, and dolphins, are a kind of sea-horse, a large papal umbrella, a crowned eagle, two versions of a caryatid or herm, and a border ornament with a human face. The volumes appear to have been issued in the peculiar order of 4, 1, 2, 3. They came to the Bodleian as early as 1659 among John Selden's books.

On: M. MUTA, *Capitulorum regni Siciliae*, 4 vols., Panormi, apud Erasmum de Simeone (I. A. de Franciscis), 1603–14.
4°, 290 × 200 × 25–30 mm. Red morocco. All edges gilt and those of vol 1 gauffered as well.
Provenance: J. Selden (1659).

PLATE XLII BODLEIAN (B 1. 23–26 Jur. Seld.)

190 POLISH PRESENTATION BINDING FOR THE BODLEIAN
Danzig, 1647

An inscribed presentation copy given to the Bodleian in 1649 by the author who later sent other works through the agency of Henry Oldenburg, one of the secretaries of the Royal Society. Hevelius (1611–81) was the founder of lunar topography, catalogued 1,564 stars, made observations of sunspots, discovered four comets, and suggested the revolution of such bodies in parabolic paths round the sun. The *Selenographia* is his main work.

On: J. HEVELIUS, *Selenographia, sive Lunae descriptio*, Gedani, autoris sumptibus, typis Hünefeldianis, 1647.
Folio, 360 × 220 × 64 mm. Red morocco.
See: W. D. Macray, *Annals of the Bodleian Library*, (1890), p. 134.
Provenance: Presented by the author 1649.

BODLEIAN (fol. BS. 62)

191 INLAID *POINTILLÉ* BINDING
Paris, *c.* 1635

This binding, the inlaid mosaic covers of which were mounted and repaired (some parts being substituted) probably in the late nineteenth century, came originally from the workshop of an unknown master gilder active in Paris between 1622 and 1638. The standard of the work of this shop after 1630 is lower than that before and changes again in 1638 when it may have been taken over by Padeloup the elder.

On: Novum Testamentum, Lutetiae, ex officina Roberti Stephani, 1550.
Folio, 357 × 230 × 40 mm. Red inlaid morocco, mounted and much repaired in the nineteenth century.
Provenance: Jacobus Corbinelli (1535-88) (signature on title-page).

PLATE XLIII ST. JOHN'S COLLEGE

Paris, *c.* 1640

The *pointillé*, or small dotted tool, here forms the background to a late fanfare design. This style of binding and any version of small head tool have commonly been ascribed to a binder called 'Le Gascon' and to Florimond Badier, but there is little to identify the former and the latter was only apprenticed in 1630. There are five versions of the head tool, which seems to have been used up to 1660 and perhaps particularly by the friends of the Chancellor Séguier (1588-1672). The tool on this binding is of Dacier's type A and is found on the best bindings of this style.

On: La Saincte Bible françoise, 3 vols., Paris, J. Richet et P. Chevalier, 1621.
 Folio, 422 × 274 × 47 mm. Red morocco.
See: T. F. Dibdin, *Bibliographical Decameron*, 2 (1817), p. 497; E. Dacier, 'Une reliure française du XVIIe siècle à la bibliothèque Bodléienne', *Le Bibliophile* (1931), pp. 55–63 and plate; Dacier, 'Autour de Le Gascon et de Florimond Badier', *Trésors des bibliothèques de France*, IV, pp. 177–86, no. 26; Philip, plate 19.
Provenance: J. B. Colbert; Count Hoym (whose arms are an addition to the original binding); Bellanger; Duc de Lamoignon; Payne; F. Douce (1834).

BODLEIAN (Douce B subt. 14)

193 DUTCH *POINTILLÉ* BINDING   Amsterdam? *c.* 1665

This volume bears a fine inscription, possibly from the translator, L. van Bos, a Dordrecht schoolmaster, to one Van der Voort, apparently the local Mayor. The style of binding in *pointillé* might have suggested that it was bound by the great Amsterdam firm of Magnus who specialized, amongst other things, in books of Jewish interest, but the bird and vine roll here is different from either of the two it is known to have used.

On: F. JOSEPHUS, *Des-wijdt vermaerden Joodschen historieschrijvers boecken*, Dordrecht, Jacobus Savry, 1665.
 Folio, 302 × 222 × 70 mm. Red morocco.
See: BFAC, plate CI.
Provenance: Van der Voort; T. R. Buchanan (1941).

PLATE XLIV   BODLEIAN (Buchanan c.3)

194 BINDING FOR THE FUTURE POPE CLEMENT X

Rome, 1669

A fairly typical Roman binding of the period, combining the elements of the fanfare, centre and corner, and fan styles. Apparently bound for Cardinal Emilio Altieri (1590–1676) who became Pope on 29 Apr. 1670. Although a tool on this binding is also to be found on one for Queen Christina of Sweden there seems to be no conclusive proof that this binding comes from the Rospigliosi or papal bindery which produced so much of the best contemporary Roman work (see S. G. Lindberg, 'Queen Christina bindings', in *Queen Christina of Sweden, documents and studies* (1966), no. 81).

On: P. MAGALLANUS, *Tractatuum theologicorum ad primam partem divi Thomae*, Ulyssipone, ex typographia Ioannis a Costa senioris 1669.
Folio, 295 × 190 × 47 mm. Red morocco.
Provenance: Pope Clement X; H. W. Chandler; presented by Mrs. M. S. Evans, 1889.

PEMBROKE COLLEGE

195 INLAID DUTCH *POINTILLÉ* BINDING   Antwerp, *c.* 1640

Small inlaid binding showing *pointillé*-style tooling used in a restricted manner with semi-circular ornaments to break up the rectangular design.

On: Officium Beatae Mariae Virginis, Antverpiae, ex officina Plantiniana, apud Baltasarem & Ioannem Moretos, 1616.
8°, 186 × 115 × 42 mm. Red morocco with inlays of citron morocco.
Provenance: G. Clarke (1736).

WORCESTER COLLEGE

196 PLAIN *POINTILLÉ* BINDING   Paris, *c.* 1630

Simple *pointillé* binding with typical central arrangement, here inlaid. Very similar bindings were made for Herbert de Montmor (1600–79) and are described by Hobson, *French*, p. 81. This book was possibly bound for a member of the Caumartin family, whose bookplate it bears, perhaps François Le Fèvre de Caumartin (1668–1733), Bishop of Blois, in whose library is known to have been a large number of *pointillé* bindings, including some with head tools.

On: R. BELLARMINE, *De ascensione mentis in deum*, Coloniae Agrippinae, apud Cornel. ab Egmond, 1626.
    16°, 110 × 50 × 16 mm. Red morocco.
See: Philip, plate 18.
Provenance: Caumartin; L. B. Guerard de la Quesnerie; S. Gibson (1950).

BODLEIAN (Gibson 15a)

197 LATE *POINTILLÉ* BINDING   Paris, 1680

A late example still using strapwork for the design and even including a fanfare-style volute tool. Very similar bindings are known on the 1644 and 1661 editions of the same work and are attributed to Antoine Ruette (born 1609), royal bookbinder from 1648 to 1664, who published both editions (see Hobson, *Fanfare*, p. 64, and Nixon, *Broxbourne*, p. 141).

On: Office de la semaine sainte, Paris, chez Charles Fosset, [1680].
    8°, 190 × 125 × 35 mm. Red morocco.
Provenance: T. R. Buchanan (1941).

BODLEIAN (Buchanan e.70)

198 *POINTILLÉ* BINDING WITH SMALL HEAD TOOL
Paris, 1647

The fanfare-style binding has here been adapted to take *pointillé* tooling which includes the small human head tool (Dacier type B) discussed under no. 192. This binding bears the arms and mono-grams of Nicolas de Bailleul, Surintendant des finances, to whom the book was dedicated. It may have been bound by, or for, Pierre Rocolet, the publisher, who probably maintained a bindery and certainly supplied Cardinal Mazarin with bound works.

112

On: N. Guillebert, *Les cent-cinquante pseaumes de David paraphrasez,*
Paris, chez Pierre Rocolet, 1647.
8°, 182 × 122 × 40 mm. Light brown morocco.
See: Dacier references under no. 192.
Provenance: N. de Bailleul; M. Montagu (1863).

PLATE XLV   BODLEIAN (Montagu 508)

199 PARISIAN BINDING FOR EVELYN'S FATHER-IN-LAW
Paris, *c.* 1650

Despite its English origin this small book was probably bound in Paris
for Sir Richard Browne (1605–83), King's Resident at the Court of
France from 1641 to 1660 and John Evelyn's father-in-law. The monogram is made up from Browne's initials together with those of his
wife (see Sir G. Keynes, *John Evelyn* (1937), pp. 25–28). The *S fermé*
(see no. 100) was by now rather old-fashioned.

On: Preces privatae in studiosorum gratiam collectae, Londini, Gullielmus
Seres, 1573.
16°, 105 × 72 × 25 mm. Black morocco.
Provenance: Sir R. Browne; F. Douce (1834).

BODLEIAN (Douce BB 7)

200 ARMORIAL BINDING   France, *c.* 1650

Bound for Adrien Poërier, baron d'Amfreville, who was Président
du Parlement de Rouen from 1657.

On: D. Petau, *Paraphrasis Psalmorum,* Parisiis, apud Sebastianum
Cramoisy, 1637.
12°, 147 × 86 × 45 mm. Light brown calf.
Provenance: Poërier; C. N. Davis; Archbishop Wake (1736).

CHRIST CHURCH

201 BOUND WITH THE ARMS OF LORRAINE   Paris, 1636

Armorial binding for an unidentified member of the Lorraine
family, sometimes suggested as being Françoise Renée de Lorraine,

marquise de Guise (1621–82). Louis Jacob in his *Traicté des plus belles bibliothèques* (1644) speaks highly of the library of the Dukes of Lorraine, 'laquelle est abondante en bons & rares livres, qui ont esté mis avec de grands soings'. For other bindings for members of the Lorraine family see nos. 102, 104, 205.

On: D. Petau, *Rationarum temporum*, Parisiis, sumptibus Sebastiani Cramoisy, 1636.
8°, 178 × 110 × 62 mm. Olive calf.
Provenance: Lorraine family; Barnard catal. July 1908, no. 26; I. Bywater (1914).

BODLEIAN (Byw. R 1.1)

202 FAN BINDING   Antwerp, *c.* 1620

The fan style was popular throughout Europe in the seventeenth century and particularly so in Italy and the Low Countries. The armorial stamp is that of Bertrand d'Eschaux (1556–1641), Archbishop of Tours.

On: N. Orlandinus, *Historiae societatis Iesu*, Antverpiae, apud filios Martini Nutii, 1620.
Folio, 343 × 210 × 60 mm. Light brown calf.
Provenance: B. d'Eschaux; Archbishop Wake (1736).

CHRIST CHURCH

203 FAN BINDING   Paris, *c.* 1630

A fan-style binding with the armorial stamp of Henri La Jomarière de Daillon, Comte and later Duc de Lude (1623—85), a close personal friend of Louis XIV and a well-known figure at Court.

On: Julian, Emperor of Rome, *Opera*, Parisiis, sumptibus Sebastiani Cramoisy, 1630.
4°, 250 × 180 × 60 mm. Light brown calf.
Provenance: de Daillon; I. Bywater (1914).

BODLEIAN (Byw. F 2.18)

FAN BINDING POSSIBLY FOR ARCHBISHOP LAUD
Netherlands? 1639

Two identical copies of this two-volume work came to Oxford through Laud's agency, one going to his newly opened library at St. John's, the other to the Bodleian (MS. Laud Misc. 303, 304). They would appear to come from the same bindery employed to cover other Laudian gifts of a continental provenance given the previous year (see Bodleian Library, *Summary Catalogue of Western Manuscripts*, II, pt. 1, p. 16). Another copy in an identical binding was in the A. F. Didot collection and is reproduced by G. Brunet in *La reliure ancienne et moderne* (1878), plate 75.

On: [P. PITHOU], *Traité des droits et libertez de l'église gallicane*, [Rouen], 1639.
Folio, 420 × 286 × 68 mm. Red morocco.
Provenance: Archbishop Laud (1634).

ST. JOHN'S COLLEGE

205 ARMORIAL BINDING   Paris, *c.* 1640

Bound with an unusual number of exterior rolls and reduced fan decoration for Nicolas François de Lorraine (1609–70), Bishop of Toul and Cardinal, who left the Church in 1634 when he became Duke and married. Subsequently persecuted by Richelieu, he had to leave Lorraine for a few years.

On: ARISTOTLE, *Opera*, Basileae, per Ioannem Hervagium, 1563.
Folio, 312 × 211 × 101 mm. Light brown calf.
Provenance: Nicolas François de Lorraine; presented by W. Jackson, 1893.

KEBLE COLLEGE

206 ROYAL DEDICATION BINDING   Paris, 1665

Bound with the arms of Philippe de France, Duc d'Orleans and brother of Louis XIV (1640–1701), to whom the book is dedicated.

On: M. DE LOS REYES, *Breve tratado de rançon de estado*, Paris, 1665.
4°, 264 × 202 × 17 mm. Red morocco.
Provenance: Duc d'Orleans.

ALL SOULS COLLEGE

207 ARMORIAL PRIZE BINDING   Toulouse, 1634?

Bound with the arms of Charles de Montchal, Archbishop of Toulouse (1628–51), and presented as a prize for rhetoric at the Jesuit College in Toulouse in 1634 to Antoine de Bourdeaux. Louis Jacob speaks in his *Traicté des plus belles bibliothèques* (1644) of Montchal's great erudition 'laquelle il puize de ces excellens livres qu'il a depuis longtemps ramassez, pour dresser cette belle bibliothèque qu'il possède'.

> *On:* L. Cresollius, *Vacationes autumnales, Sive De perfecta orationis actione et pronunciatione libri III*, Lutetiae Parisiorum, ex officina Nivelliana sumptibus Sebastiani Cramoisy, 1620.
> 4°, 238 × 174 × 45 mm. Red morocco.
> *Provenance:* A. de Bourdeaux.

All Souls College

208 ARMORIAL BINDING   Paris, 1623

Fan-style armorial binding with the arms of Thomas II de Morand, baron de Mesnil-Garnier (1584–1651), who was Commandeur et Grand Trésorier des Ordres du Roi from 1621 to 1633. His library is also mentioned in Jacob's *Traicté des plus belles bibliothèques* (1644).

> *On:* Nonnus of Panoplis, *Paraphrasis sancti secundum Joannem evangelii*, Parisiis, sumptibus Sebastiani Cramoisy, 1623.
> 8°, 178 × 108 × 25 mm. Red morocco.
> *Provenance:* de Morand; J. Asselin (bookplate).

All Souls College

209 PLAIN *POINTILLÉ* BINDING   Paris, 1638

In 1638 John Scudamore, the English ambassador in Paris, tried to export a manuscript of the Emperor Basil's laws but was prevented from doing so by Richelieu. The present work was translated the same year by his son and this copy was probably bound in Paris. Two of the tools are probably identical with some on a binding presented to Richelieu in 1636 (see Hobson, *French*, p. 82).

On: Basil I, Emperor of the East, *The sixty sixe admonitory chapters*,
Printed at Paris, 1638.
8°, 178 × 112 × 18 mm. Red morocco.
Provenance: E. Wathan 1755; B. Quaritch Ltd., catal. 776, item 59.

Bodleian (Vet. E 2 e. 28)

210 ARMORIAL BINDING   Paris, 1670

Bound with the arms and monogram of Elie du Fresnoy (1614–98)
who was Premier commis to the Chancelier Le Tellier, and then to
the Marquis de Louvois. Du Fresnoy seems to have kept to the same
style of binding, popular in his youth, throughout his life.

On: Polybius, *Historiarum libri qui supersunt,* Amstelodami, ex officina
Johannis Janssonii à Waesbergae et Johannis a Someren, 1670.
8°, 190 × 112 × 50 mm. Red morocco.
See: BFAC, no. 70.
Provenance: du Fresnoy; A. Atherley; T. R. Buchanan (1941).

Bodleian (Buchanan e. 71)

211 PLAIN *POINTILLÉ* BINDING   Paris, 1635

Plain *pointillé* binding with empty central oval. The exterior rolls
were all popular throughout the seventeenth century.

On: Apuleius, *Apologia*, Parisiis, apud Simoneum Ferier, 1635.
4°, 254 × 180 × 32 mm. Red morocco.
Provenance: G. Clarke (1736).

Worcester College

THE GREAT AGE OF ENGLISH DECORATIVE BINDING

During the Commonwealth new and gayer colours for morocco, particularly the red 'Turkey' leather, were introduced into England simultaneously with new tools and designs. Although greatly influenced by continental, and especially French, work, English binders adopted much more naturalistic floral and foliate tools, notably combined in a sort of volute, and often used massed together as in nos. 219–21. While tulips, poppies, roses, acorns and thistles were common, birds and animals were rare. Another characteristic tool of the period is the so-called drawer-handle, very prominent in nos. 236–8, but which was also used in the Netherlands. The general design of the period evolved from the inner panel which was broken first at the centre of the sides, then at the top and bottom where the lines, inclined outwards, gave the effect of the architectural 'broken pediment' or, as it is usually known, the 'cottage roof' style.

At one time, the majority of these richly decorated bindings were ascribed to Samuel Mearne, bookbinder to Charles II, and, though nos. 217–22 came from his bindery, much distinguished work was produced in London by such men as Richard Balley (no. 230), Daniel Search (no. 229), and unidentified shops like the 'Queens' binders' (no. 237–40).

Binders also flourished in Oxford and produced some fine college Benefactors' Registers (nos. 215, 224–6, 231, 233) and on presentation volumes (no. 223), while their more ordinary work on devotional books, such as no. 228, was equally of a high standard.

212 BOUND BY THE ROYAL HEADS BINDER London? c. 1665

A typical red morocco binding with black and citron onlays from a shop which was active early in Charles II's reign. It bound a certain number of service books for royal use, and on two anthem books in the Chapel Royal occur the eponymous tools which portray Charles II and his Queen. None of the printed books decorated with this group of tools has an imprint later than 1664 and it has been suggested that this binder's equipment may have been lost in the Fire of London in 1666.

On: Sir William Waller's Apology, autograph fair copy.
　　264 × 170 × 18 mm. Red morocco, black and citron onlays.
See: Friends of the Bodleian, *Thirteenth annual report, 1937–38,* p. 19;
　　Book Collector, XVII (1968), p. 44.
Provenance: Thomas Wood; C. H. St. John Hornby; presented by
　　him through the Friends of the Bodleian, 1938.

PLATE XLVI　　　　　　　　　　　　　BODLEIAN (MS. Don. d.57)

213　BOUND BY THE ROYAL HEADS BINDER London? *c.* 1665

This binding comes from the same shop as no. 212, with a similar
design and many tools common to both. The manuscript is unfortunately imperfect; it contains cookery recipes written in several
hands from about 1665 and was presumably used in a noble household, since names of contributors are occasionally given, such as
Lord Alford, Lord Capel, and Lord Conway.

On: Manuscript book of cookery recipes, used *c.* 1665–1710.
　　308 × 196 × 11 mm. Red morocco, black and citron onlays.
See: *Book Collector,* XVII (1968), p. 44.
Provenance: Unknown; in the College before 1852.

EXETER COLLEGE (MS. 71)

214　A LONDON BINDING　　　　　　London, *c.* 1670

The elaboration by decoration of the rectangular panels found on
early seventeenth-century books can be seen on the example shown
here. The practice of breaking the tops and sides of the inner rectangle is also demonstrated, but this binding favours a circular design
rather than the 'cottage roof' effect.

On: CHARLES I, *Workes,* London, James Flesher for R. Royston, 1662.
　　Folio, 357 × 214 × 50 mm. Black morocco, original back.
Provenance: Unknown; in the College in the nineteenth century.

ORIEL COLLEGE

I　　　　　　　　　　　119

This finely bound volume is an example of the sumptuous benefactors' registers commissioned by Oxford colleges in the late seventeenth century (see also nos. 219, 224–6, 231, 233). It appears, to judge from the tools, to be the work of the same binder who bound nos. 231 and 232 but other evidence makes ascription difficult. Richard Webb, a binder at work in Oxford between about 1672 and 1721, is mentioned in the Corpus Christi College accounts between 1682 and 1700 but the entry for 1 Jan. 1701, 'The binder's bill for binding old book and the Benefactor [*sic*]: £1 10. 6.', does not mention him by name. The same tools apparently also appear on a binding which manuscript evidence attributes to Richard Sedgley (see nos. 231–2). There were, of course, several binding shops in Oxford at this period.

The first entries in this Register were made about 1690, possibly by a scribe called Castle who was paid for writing Commemoration prayers in 1697.

On: Liber Benefactorum Collegii Corporis Christi Oxon., manuscript started *c.* 1690.
   430 × 330 × 50 mm. Red morocco.
See: Corpus Christi College accounts, *Libri magni*, 1682 (93, 95, 97, 1700).

Plate xlvii   Corpus Christi College

THE MEARNE BINDERY

The bindings on the books shown at nos. 216–22 come, according to the evidence of the tools, from the bindery of Samuel Mearne, bookbinder to Charles II from the Restoration to his death in 1683. The shop continued until about 1690. Recent research has established (Nixon, *Twelve*, pp. 58–61; *Broxbourne*, pp. 148–51, 240) the definite means of identification after E. Gordon Duff's dismissal of Cyril Davenport's wholesale attributions (C. Davenport, *Samuel Mearne, binder to King Charles II* (1906); E. G. Duff, 'The great Mearne myth', *Papers of the Edinburgh Bibliographical Society*, 1918). The numerous Bibles and Books of Common Prayer which came from this shop can be differentiated into two categories: first, those discarded at triennial intervals from the Chapels Royal, becoming the perquisites of the Clerk of the Closet (as no. 221) and, secondly, those finely bound for private persons (as no. 222).

Besides those displayed, the following books in Oxford colleges can also be ascribed to this bindery: a folio Cambridge Bible of 1660 discarded from the Chapel Royal and presented to Brasenose by John Dolben in 1666; a Bible of the same edition at Balliol, bound for John Evelyn, the diarist, with one of his armorial stamps added; a Book of Common Prayer of 1669, formerly in the Provost's stall in Queen's College chapel and now in the College library; A. Duchesne, *Historiae Francorum scriptores* (2 vols.), 1526, at Trinity; and an undistinguished but important little volume of tracts by Ridley, Latimer and others at St. John's with an inscription ending 'And bound in one volem by [space] Mearne in Pellecan Courte, in Littill Brettin, for Cor: [nelius?] Pigeon, Anno 1655'.

216   A SELECTION OF ALMANACS   London 1664–93

The printing of almanacs was a valuable monopoly of the Stationers' Company; it is not uncommon to find those for a particular year all together in a handsome binding, as here. The presence of the royal initials in palm leaves under a crown does not indicate royal ownership, but rather that they were supplied for use in what we should now call the Civil Service. The designs in this selection vary slightly from year to year, but the presence of identical tools on the 1674, 1676, 1679, 1680 and 1683 volumes reveals they were bound in the same shop. Moreover the triangular floral tool used in 1674 and

1679, together with the triangular arabesque on the almanacs for 1676, 1679, 1680, and 1683, are also found on bindings ascribed to Samuel Mearne (nos. 218–22). A roll and the royal cipher on the 1664 volume can be seen on the 1660 Bible bound by Mearne and presented to Brasenose College in 1666 by John Dolben, then Clerk of the Closet. There is also documentary evidence that Mearne bound almanacs.

On: Bound volumes of almanacs for 1664, 1674, 1675, 1676 (2 variants), 1677, 1679, 1680, 1683, 1693, London, 1664–93.
    8°, various sizes. Red morocco.
See: Nixon, *Broxbourne*, p. 151; University of London, *Historical and armorial bookbindings exhibited in the University Library* (1937), no. 11, for almanacs of 1678 ascribed to Mearne; C. Davenport, *Samuel Mearne, binder to King Charles II* (1906), pp. 62, 65.
Provenance: Bequeathed by Richard Rawlinson (1755).

BODLEIAN (Rawl. almanacs 19, 44, 46, 49, 50, 52, 58, 62, 67, 85)

217 A BINDING WITH THE ROYAL ARMS   London, *c.* 1660

The presence of the royal arms does not necessarily indicate royal ownership but rather a publisher's binding, as is the case here. Five other copies of this edition are known with exactly similar stamps, and its use was merely as a device to point to the contents. This particular stamp is similarly found on a copy of *A Collection of His Majesties Gracious Letters* (1660) in the Evelyn Collection at Christ Church, as well as on a 1661 *Book of Common Prayer* in the same College. The outer roll of circles within hoops appears to be the same as that on the volume in St. John's College, apparently bound by Mearne for Cor. Pigeon in 1655 (see the introduction to this section).

On: [J. Gauden], *Eikon Basilike*, [London, Roger Daniel], 1649.
    8°, 210 × 130 × 24 mm. Black crushed morocco, original spine.
See: C. Davenport, *Samuel Mearne, binder to King Charles II* (1906), plates 1, 4; F. F. Madan, *A new bibliography of the Eikon Basilike* (Oxford Bibliographical Society, new series III, 1950), no. 26, 2nd issue; Nixon, *Broxbourne*, p. 150.
Provenance: Unknown; in the College in the eighteenth century.

ST. JOHN'S COLLEGE

Samuel Mearne is known to have supplied many of the copies of the Statutes of the Garter issued to the Knights at their installation and the tools suggest that this is one of them. Unfortunately, the frontispiece, which would have contained the original Knight's arms, has been removed.

On: The Statutes of the Garter, manuscript, *c.* 1670.
258 × 180 × 10 mm. Black morocco, original back.
See: C. DAVENPORT, *Samuel Mearne, binder to King Charles II* (1906), p. 63; Nixon, *Broxbourne*, p. 151.
Provenance: Unknown; given to H. Smedley by Dominic Colnaghi in the nineteenth century.

ASTOR DEPOSIT (A3)

Unlike the other college benefactors' registers displayed (nos. 215, 224–26, 231, 233), which were bound in Oxford, this magnificent volume from Queen's comes from the Mearne shop in London. The tools can be seen on the other books from the same bindery; for example, the triangular floral corner-piece under a vase surmounted by Mearne's characteristic tool of a flower in a circle of leaves is very similarly used on no. 222. The volume was presented by Sir Joseph Williamson (1633–1701), sometime Secretary of State and one of the College's greatest benefactors; the upper cover has his arms on the silver centre-piece and his crest on the corner-pieces, while the lower has those of Robert Eglesfield, founder of the College. Mearne is known to have bound other books for Williamson. Another unusual feature is that the list of Williamson's numerous gifts has been signed by the scribe: 'Geo. Jeames scrips. 1680'.

On: QUEEN'S COLLEGE, Liber Albus Benefactorum, manuscript, 1680.
380 × 270 × 5 mm. Black morocco, original back.
See: C. Davenport, *Samuel Mearne, binder to King Charles II* (1906), pp. 45–46, 63; J. R. Magrath, *The Queen's College* (1921), I, p. 283; II, p. 67.
Provenance: Presented by Sir Joseph Williamson, *c.* 1680.

QUEEN'S COLLEGE

The tools reveal that this fine cottage binding comes from the shop of Samuel Mearne. Apart from the absence of tulips and poppies, the design is unusual in that the lower half of each cover does not reflect the upper; the symbolism of the flame or smoking funnel is not clear. Since there are no royal ciphers or emblems in the tooling nor on the fore-edge painting of the Crucifixion, it would appear that this Prayer Book was intended for use by a private person rather than in the Chapels Royal.

On: The Book of Common Prayer, London, Iohn Bill & Christopher Barker, (1662).
Folio, 450 × 260 × 65 mm. Red morocco, black and fawn onlays.
See: Worshipful Company of Goldsmiths *and* Oxford Society, *Treasures of Oxford* (1953), no. 221; Nixon, *Broxbourne*, p. 151; Baltimore, no. 418.
Provenance: Brooke bequest (1911).

KEBLE COLLEGE

221 A MEARNE BINDING FOR CHARLES II   London, *c*. 1669

Samuel Mearne, as the royal bookseller, supplied Bibles and Prayer Books for the use of both the King and the Chapels Royal, and these were replaced at triennial intervals when the ones for the monarch's own use became the perquisites of the Clerk of the Closet. One such volume was presented by John Dolben to Brasenose in 1666; his successor for the remainder of the reign was Nathaniel, 3rd Baron Crewe, Bishop of Durham, and Rector of Lincoln College 1668–72, and so there are several of these handsome books known which are associated with him. The one displayed was presented to Lincoln College, with its companion Bible, in 1674, and may have been the copies supplied in 1669. The royal ciphers and emblems are painted on the fore-edge as was customary in these books bound for the use of the monarch.

On: The Book of Common Prayer, London, printed by His Majesties printers, 1669.
Folio, 365 × 235 × 55 mm. Red morocco with black onlays, original spine.

See: *Book Collector*, X (1961), p. 440.
Provenance: Charles II; Nathaniel, 3rd Baron Crewe, Bishop of
  Durham; presented by him, 1674.

PLATE XLVIII   LINCOLN COLLEGE

222 FROM THE MEARNE BINDERY   London, *c.* 1670

As in no. 220, the tools on this more sombre binding reveal that it
comes from the Mearne shop. Similarly, there are no symbols of
royal ownership, while the fore-edge is only gilded, not painted.
Although the provenance of this volume is unrecorded, it was
probably intended for use by a private person or in an ordinary
church; a rather similarly bound Prayer Book of the same year is in
the Victoria and Albert Museum (see J. P. Harthan, *Bookbindings*
(Victoria and Albert Museum illustrated booklet no. 2, 1961),
plate 44).

On: *The Book of Common Prayer*, London, printed by John Bill &
  Christopher Barker, (1669).
  Folio, 374 × 242 × 50 mm. Black morocco, original back.

                                                NEW COLLEGE

OXFORD AND LATE-SEVENTEENTH CENTURY ENGLISH BINDINGS

After the Restoration the standard of bindings produced by Oxford craftsmen, like that of their London contemporaries, reached a much higher artistic level than that of the first half of the century. During this period, several colleges commissioned sumptuously bound and decorated volumes from local binders to record benefactions. Some were the work of Roger Bartlett (nos. 224–6), but others in a similar style come from other men (nos. 215, 231, 233). At the same time fine bindings were ordered for presentation purposes (no. 223), and devotional books, mainly those written by Richard Allestree (1619–81), Canon of Christ Church and Regius Professor of Divinity, received attractive covers from both Oxford and London binders (nos. 227, 228). Contemporary work by known London craftsmen, such as Daniel Search (no. 229) and Richard Balley (no. 230) is also displayed here.

223 BOUND BY THE SPANIEL BINDER   London? *c.* 1680

After the publication of Anthony Wood's *Historia Universitatis Oxoniensis* in 1674 and David Loggan's *Oxonia illustrata* in 1675, the University frequently bought specially bound copies for presentation. The Wood shown here, and its similarly bound companion by Loggan, were probably prepared in readiness for an official order that never came, for the University's achievement in the centre of each cover has been overlaid with a lozenge-shaped piece of tooled morocco. The hidden armorial stamp, with lion and Holy Lamb supporters and two mottoes, is an unusual version made by one Wilkins, a goldsmith, in 1654 (see E. A. Greening Lamborn, 'The arms of Oxford', *Oxford*, V (1938), pp. 46–48). The other binding tools show it to be the work of a binder who used an attractive spaniel ornament on an Oxford-printed Bible of 1680 now in the British Museum, but the eponymous tool is not found either on the volume displayed or on two other books from the same shop also in the Museum (see *Book Collector*, I (1952), p. 2).

On: [A. WOOD], *Historia et Antiquitates Universitatis Oxoniensis*, Oxonii e Theatro Sheldoniano, 1675.
Folio, 415 × 273 × 60 mm. Red morocco, original back.

OXFORD UNIVERSITY PRESS (Printer's Library)

Roger Bartlett, after losing his binder's shop in the Great Fire of London in 1666, migrated to Oxford where he worked until about 1690, dying in his native Watlington aged about 82 in 1712. Three of the college benefactors' books of late seventeenth-century date can be assigned to him (nos. 224–6), while he also bound presentation copies for the University authorities to give to important persons. His work has certain distinctive features, such as the row of floral volutes along the cottage roofs, and swags hanging from the eaves. This is the only Bartlett binding with lettering on the covers although it is otherwise very similar to no. 225.

On: Catalogus benefactorum Collegii B. Mariae Magdalenae Oxon., manuscript begun *c.* 1680.
   395 × 280 × 50 mm. Dark green morocco, silver clasps and chain.
See: H. M. Nixon, 'Roger Bartlett's bookbindings', *The Library*, 5th series, XVII (1962), pp. 56–57 (plate VII).

MAGDALEN COLLEGE

225 BOUND BY ROGER BARTLETT   Oxford, 1682

The style of this register of donors of plate to University College is very similar to that used by Bartlett for the Magdalen benefactors' register two years previously (no. 224), though there are neither lettering nor central side sprays here, while the colour of the morocco is crimson instead of greenish blue. University College is unusual in having three separate benefactors' registers: for plate, for general gifts (no. 233) and for gifts to the library, but only the first was bound by Bartlett, though he was well acquainted with Obadiah Walker, Master of the College.

On: Donors of plate to University College, Oxford, manuscript, begun in 1682.
   365 × 290 × 30 mm. Crimson morocco, original back.
See: I. G. Philip, 'Roger Bartlett, bookbinder', *The Library*, 5th series, X (1955), pp. 234–5, 242 (plate II); H. M. Nixon, 'Roger Bartlett's bookbindings', *The Library*, 5th series, XVII (1962), pp. 58–65.
Provenance: Bound in 1682 at a cost of 14s. (College accounts).

UNIVERSITY COLLEGE

This elaborately decorated volume was purchased in 1685, and from the evidence of the tools can be ascribed to Roger Bartlett. The decoration in cottage style, with swags hanging from the eaves, is similar to that of the Magdalen and University College registers (nos. 224–5), except for the massed small tools in the centres which are more reminiscent of his bindings on smaller devotional books. The College had spent £4 8s. on this by May 1685, presumably on the binding and the writing of the inscriptions by one 'Mr. Clerk'.

On: The Book of Benefactors of St. Edmund Hall, manuscript begun
    c. 1685.
    380 × 272 × 35 mm. Crimson morocco with black onlays,
    original back.
See: A. B. Emden, *An account of the chapel and library building of St.*
    Edmund Hall (1932), pp. 13–14 (plates 2, 3); Hobson, *English,*
    56; I. G. Philip, 'Roger Bartlett, bookbinder', *The Library,* 5th
    series, X (1955), pp. 241–2 (plate IV); H. M. Nixon, 'Roger
    Bartlett's bookbindings', *The Library,* 5th series, XVII (1962),
    p. 58.

ST. EDMUND HALL

227 AN ENGLISH RESTORATION BINDING   London? *c.* 1678

Many copies of the various devotional works by Richard Allestree, author of *The whole duty of man* (1659), are found in bindings with elaborate overall decoration and were evidently intended for gifts. This is a typical example by an unidentified craftsman. Common tools of the period, such as drawer-handles, tulips, and various leaves are prominent, but the unusual feature of this binding lies in the use of alternating coloured onlays in the centre- and corner-pieces.

On: [R. ALLESTREE], *The ladies calling,* 4th impression, at the Theater
    in Oxford, 1676.
    4°, 118 × 111 × 24 mm. Red, black and green morocco, original
    back.
Provenance: Frances Jackson; John M. Traherne; S. Gibson (1949).

BODLEIAN (Gibson 87)

Besides specially commissioned work, such as the benefactors' registers (nos. 224–6), Bartlett also bound more ordinary books like the one displayed here which has not previously been recorded. It is very similar in style to another copy of the same devotional work formerly in the possession of Major J. R. Abbey, where tulips are used above and below the centre-piece instead of the poppies found here (see Hobson, *English*, p. 56 (no. 41); Sotheby & Co., 21 June 1965, lot 11 (plate 2)).

On: [R. ALLESTREE], *The ladies calling*, Oxford, printed at the Theater, 1673.
  4°, 183 × 116 × 22 mm. Blue morocco, original back.
Provenance: Anne Wharton, 1673; Sarah FitzJames, 1678; Eliza Taylor; James Ingram; bequeathed by him, 1850.

PLATE XLIX   TRINITY COLLEGE

229 POSSIBLY BOUND BY DANIEL SEARCH   London, *c.* 1692

This characteristic binding, with red onlays decorated with floral and filigree tooling, was possibly the work of Daniel Search, who was at work in London during the reigns of James II, William III and Mary (see Nixon, *Twelve*, p. 63). There are four different patterns on the panels on the spine, while under the gilt on the fore-edge is painted a floral design with 'Search the Scriptures 1692'.

On: Holy Bible, London, by the assigns of John Bill deceas'd, and by Henry Hills, and Thomas Newcomb, 1682; *New Testament*, London, John Bill, Thomas Newcomb and Henry Hills, 1679; *Whole book of Psalms*, London, printed for the Company of Stationers, 1692.
  4°, 195 × 124 × 45 mm. Black morocco, with onlaid centre-piece, corner-pieces and flowers, original back.
See: Philip, plate 21.
Provenance: Mary Oliver; William S. Gilby, 1839; S. Gibson (1949).

PLATE L   BODLEIAN (Gibson 77)

According to Bagford, Richard Balley had been taught by Suckerman during his apprenticeship in Samuel Mearne's shop and was one of those who 'ought to be remembered in after ages'. The design of the binding shown here is practically identical with that on a backless binding formerly owned by Major J. R. Abbey, except that this one has only a narrow outer border of fillets and dots, while onlaid cinquefoils are used instead of closed tulips. For details of the work of this binder see Hobson, *English,* p. 80 (no. 61); Nixon, *Twelve,* p. 60; *Book Collector,* IV (1955), p. 144; Sotheby & Co., 21 June 1965, lot 218 (plate 27).

On: The Book of Common Prayer, London, Charles Bill and the executrix of Thomas Newcomb deceas'd, 1695; *Whole book of Psalms,* London, W. and J. Wilde for the Company of Stationers, 1696. 8°, 190 × 120 × 35 mm. Black morocco, red and fawn onlays, silver corners, original back.
Provenance: H. P. Liddon; bequeathed by him, 1890.

KEBLE COLLEGE

231 POSSIBLY BOUND BY RICHARD SEDGLEY

Oxford, *c.* 1692

The cottage design went out of fashion before the end of the seventeenth century, though the square shape of the volume shown here would possibly not have been suitable for one. The typical floral motifs can be seen on the tools used, while the wide outer border, made by the double use of the same roll, is unusual. Pembroke College employed Roger Bartlett until at least 1683, but this volume has not been found mentioned in the College accounts. The tools are the same as those on nos. 215 and 232, on the benefactors' register of St. Mary Hall (now at Oriel College) of about 1688, and on a large paper volume of tracts by Aldrich and others, all printed in Oxford in 1687 or 1688 and now at Christ Church. All these are probably the work of Richard Sedgley, who bound in Oxford from 1686 and on his death in 1719 (aged 72) was described by Hearne as 'an extraordinary good binder'.

On: Liber benefactorū Coll: Pemb: Oxon., manuscript begun *c.* 1692.

    415 × 360 × 30 mm. Red morocco, original back.

See: T. Hearne, *Remarks and Collections,* VII (Oxford Hist. Soc., XLVIII, 1906), p. 58.

PEMBROKE COLLEGE

232   POSSIBLY BOUND BY RICHARD SEDGLEY
Oxford? c. 1690

Another example of the same binder as nos. 215 and 231. The style, with swags hanging from cottage eaves, is reminiscent of Roger Bartlett, who on his retirement about 1690 presumably left Sedgley as Oxford's finest binder.

On: Ἡ Καινὴ Διαθήκη, ᾽Εκ Βασιλικῆς τυπογράφιας ἐν Παρίσιοις, 1642.

    Folio, 442 × 307 × 45 mm. Dark blue morocco, original back.

Provenance: Unknown: in the College by the early nineteenth century.

PLATE LI   EXETER COLLEGE

233   BENEFACTORS' REGISTER BY AN UNKNOWN BINDER
Oxford? c. 1690

The craftsman who finished this fine cottage binding is unknown. Some of the tools, such as the large carnation at the central sides, are very close to those used by Bartlett, but the unequally placed drawer-handles round the ten lozenges in the central compartment betray a lower standard and, unlike Roger Bartlett's work, the roof is made from only a roll and fillet, nor is it decorated with volutes.

On: General benefactors' register, manuscript begun *c.* 1690.

    380 × 285 × 40 mm. Red morocco, original back.

UNIVERSITY COLLEGE

OTHER LATE SEVENTEENTH-CENTURY
ENGLISH BINDINGS

The elaborate and attractive bindings that first appeared during the Commonwealth and were developed after the Restoration, continued into the reign of Queen Anne with little change. The great variations of design made possible by the use of small individual tools are well exemplified here. Drawer-handle tools are prominent in nos. 236–8, while the effective combination of flowers and leaves, some formal and others naturalistic, can be seen in the other bindings displayed.

234 BOUND BY ROBERT STEELE   London, 1693

Like Balley (no. 230), Steele also served his apprenticeship in Samuel Mearne's shop and was later in business on his own from about 1677 to 1710. John Dunton, the bookseller, in his *Life and Errors*, called him his 'occasional binder' whose fine work vied with that of the better Cambridge binders. Six copies of these special forms of prayer were normally supplied bound in Turkey leather for the Closet— the royal family's private gallery pew—and twelve for use in the main Chapel Royal at Whitehall (see Baltimore, no. 42).

On: A form of prayer and thanksgiving for the preservation of His Majesty and for his safe return to his people, London, Charles Bill and the executrix of Thomas Newcomb deceas'd, 1693.
    4°, 202 × 150 × 6 mm. Red morocco, original back.
Provenance: King William III; Judith English, 1714; 'G.V.N. no. 35'.

ASTOR DEPOSIT (C10)

235 AN ENGLISH RESTORATION BINDING   London? *c.* 1678

The binder of this French version of the Book of Common Prayer has not been identified. The curves in the pattern, usually made by drawer-handle tools at this period, are here effected by fillets.

On: La liturgie de l'Eglise Anglicane, Londres, pour Robert Scott &
se vend chez Geo. Wells, & Sam. Cart, 1678.
8°, 153 × 92 × 28 mm. Black morocco with red onlays, original
back.
Provenance: Brooke bequest (1911).

KEBLE COLLEGE

**236 RESTORATION BINDING WITH DRAWER-HANDLE
TOOLING**   London, *c.* 1680

This binding is an unusual variation of the overall repetitive pattern
associated with the use of drawer-handle tools in that the centre-
and side-pieces have been made up of small tools in an adaptation
of the centre-piece style. This binding is very similar to one in the
Broxbourne Library on a copy of *The ladies calling* of 1677, but it has
none of the latter's distinctive tools (see Nixon, *Broxbourne*, pp. 158–9).

On: PETRUS RIGA, Aurora; poema, manuscript, written in the late
twelfth century.
195 × 120 × 29 mm. Black morocco, blue onlays, original back.
Provenance: R. Rawlinson (1755).

BODLEIAN (MS. Rawl. C. 819)

237 BOUND BY THE QUEENS' BINDER B   London, *c.* 1675

Catherine of Braganza and Mary of Modena owned bindings
thought at one time to have been the work of one craftsman, whom
G. D. Hobson designated the 'Queens' binder'. Subsequent research
has shown the work to have come from at least four shops. The binding shown here and no. 238 are the work of Queens' binder B, whose
standards were usually higher than those of Queens' binder A (nos.
239–40). For details of the work of the Queens' binder B see Hobson,
Cambridge, pp. 144–5 (plate LVIII); Baltimore, nos. 416–17; *Book
Collector*, VIII (1959), p. 50.

On: [R. ALLSTREE], *The government of the tongue*, at the Theater in
Oxford, 1675.
4°, 186 × 112 × 17 mm. Dark blue morocco, original back.
Provenance: William Roberts; Ellen Hamilton; S. Gibson (1949).

PLATE LII   BODLEIAN (Gibson 85)

238 BOUND BY THE QUEENS' BINDER B   London, *c.* 1683

The volume shown is a fine example of the high standards reached by the Queens' binder B. The breaking up of the overall drawer-handle tool design by means of a lozenge frame is also used on a volume in New York Public Library.

On: Orders and letters to Admiral A. Herbert, 1672–83, manuscript.
    350 × 225 × 38 mm. Black morocco, original back.
See: Philip, plate 20.
Provenance: R. Rawlinson (1755).

BODLEIAN (MS. Rawl. A. 228)

239 BOUND BY THE QUEENS' BINDER A   London, *c.* 1680

The Queens' binder A had a very large output during the 1670s and 1680s and his standards vary widely, probably indicating that more than one finisher was employed. The smaller volumes from this shop have an overall design with drawer-handle tools prominent, but on the larger books, such as the one shown here, an interesting ribbon on the fanfare pattern was sometimes favoured. For details of the work of the Queens' binder A see Hobson, *Cambridge*, pp. 144–5 (plate LVIII); Baltimore, nos. 414–15; *Book Collector*, XII (1963), p. 488. Recently Mr. Nixon has tentatively identified the Queens' binder A as William Nott, a craftsman of high repute of whom Samuel Pepys wrote: 'To Nott's the famous bookbinder, that bound for my Lord Chancellor's library: there did I take occasion for curiosity to bespeak a book to be bound, only that I might have one of his binding.' (Hobson, *Cambridge*, pp. 164–5).

On: M. F. QUINTILIANUS, *De institutione oratoria*, Parisiis, apud Vascosanum, 1549.
    Folio, 320 × 220 × 44 mm. Red morocco, original back.
Provenance: Henry Aldrich; bequeathed by him, 1710.

CHRIST CHURCH

240 BOUND BY THE QUEENS' BINDER A   London, 1688

Although this binder usually applied an interlacing ribbon pattern to large books, it could be used on smaller ones in special cases such

134

as the volume displayed here. This was a presentation copy to the Queen Dowager, Catherine of Braganza, so the royal achievement was necessary in the first instance, ribbon patterns being added to complete the decoration. The armorial stamp is also used on a volume by the same binder now in the British Museum.

On: R. HUDLESTON, *A short and plain way to the faith and church,* London, Henry Hills, 1688.

4°, 200 × 155 × 10 mm. Red morocco.
Provenance: Queen Catherine of Braganza.

ASTOR DEPOSIT (C8)

INDEX OF AUTHORS

References are to item numbers

K*

INDEX OF BINDERS

References are to item numbers

INDEX OF PREVIOUS OWNERS

References are to item numbers

Ailain, Madame 88
Aldrich, H. 131, 239
Allestree, R. 164
Altieri, E. *see* Clement X, Pope
Anne of Austria 183
Asselin, J. 208
Atherley, A. 210
Bacon, F. 135, 170, 172
Bailleul, N. de 198
Banks, J. C. 76
Barat 106
Barberini, A. Cardinal 187
Bellanger 192
Berbonsier, A. 41
Bernard, E. 77
Berri, M. C., Duchesse de 98
Berry, M. 92
Bindley, J. 57
Bodley, Sir T. 127
Boersburgh, U. von 115
Bono, M. 8, 10
Bos, L. van 193
Boucher, J. 114
Bourdeaux, A. de 207
Bourlamaque, C. C. de 34
Brabazon, W. J. M. 186
Brand, J. 146, 153
Bridgewater, J. Egerton, 1st Earl of 146
Brodeau, J. 101
Brooke, C. E. and T. 1, 19, 34, 95, 98,
　　133, 220, 235
Browne, Sir R. 199
Buchanan, T. R. 5, 28, 102, 184, 188,
　　193, 197, 210
Buckeridge, J. 126
Buckingham, G. Villiers, Duke of 136,
　　137, 173
Burghley, M. Cecil, Baroness 72
Burghley, W. Cecil, 1st Baron 125
Burn, J. H. 48
Buti, R. 6
Bywater, I. 201, 203
Caen: Jesuit college 81
Cahill, J. B. 89
Calanacci 3

Canonici, M. L. 3, 11
Carpender, W. 118
Carrara, F. da 9
Catherine of Braganza 240
Caumartin family 196
Chandler, H. W. 104, 194
Charles I 142, 143, 148, 155
Charles II 144, 158, 221
Chartres: Cathedral library 104
Chauncy, C. 29, 35, 176
Cheffault 27
Cherry, F. 162
Chesterfield, Earls of 73
Cisternay du Fay, C. J. 38
Clarke, B. 121
Clarke, G. and W. 13, 141, 143, 144, 145,
　　148, 152, 155, 158, 183, 195, 211
Clayton, T. 116
Clement X, Pope 194
Colbert 192
Cole, H. 65
Coleraine, H., 3rd Baron 22
Colnaghi, D. 218
Coningsby, G. 59, 72
Corbinelli, J. 191
Cranebrooke, S. de 126
Crawford, W. H. 18
Crewe, N., 3rd Baron 221
Crouchman, J. 74
Crynes, N. 125
Daillon, H. de 203
Davis, C. N. 200
Deleen, W. 66
Denbigh, B. Feilding, 4th Earl of 136
Dent, J. 38
Douce, F. 24, 25, 29, 31, 32, 35, 38, 42,
　　50, 51, 53, 55, 58, 64, 79, 82, 88, 114,
　　138, 149, 163, 175, 176, 182, 192, 199
Douglas, Sir W. F. 5
Drury, H. 9
Du Chatelet, P. 79
Du Fresnoy, E. 210
Duodo, P. 92-4
Du Saix, A. 25
Du Vivier, J. 90

INDEX OF BODLEIAN BOOKS
by shelfmarks

PLATE I

5. Italian binding with device, Bologna, *c.* 1540

BODLEIAN

PLATE II

10. Ducale issued to Michael Bono, Venice, 1572

PLATE III

11. Bound for Nicolao Franco, Bishop of Treviso, Venice, *c.* 1490

BODLEIAN

PLATE IV

15. Presentation binding for Alfonso d'Este, Venice, 1559

MAGDALEN COLLEGE

PLATE V

27. Bound for François I, Paris, 1537

PLATE VI

29. French trade binding, Paris, *c.* 1540
BODLEIAN

PLATE VII

32. Bound by Plantin for Henri II, Paris, 1549

BODLEIAN

PLATE VIII

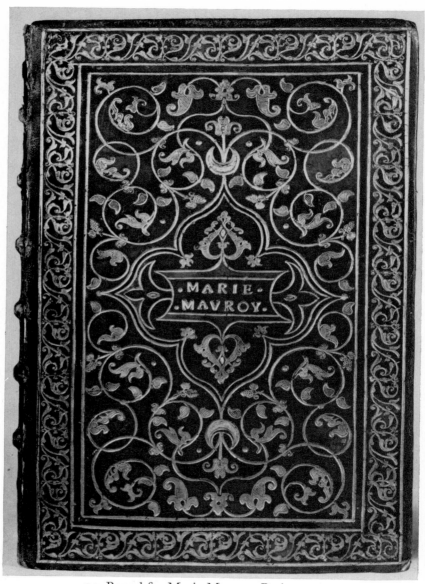

34. Bound for Marie Mauroy, Paris, *c.* 1550
KEBLE COLLEGE

PLATE IX

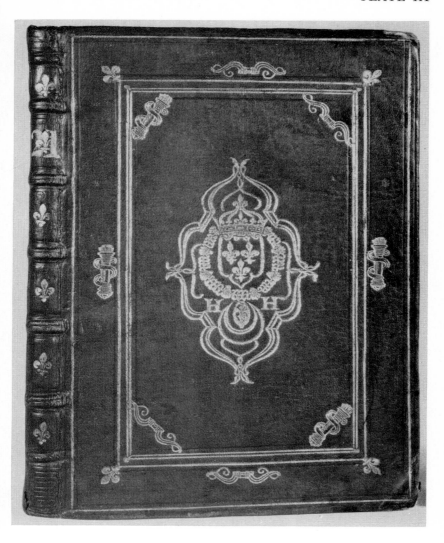

36. Official binding with the arms of Henri II, *c.* 1550
BODLEIAN

PLATE X

40. Greek style binding from Paris, *c.* 1550
BALLIOL COLLEGE

PLATE XI

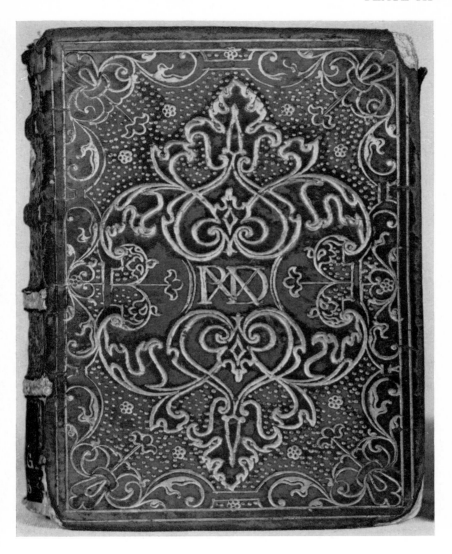

41. By the Binder of the Estienne Bible, *c.* 1540
BODLEIAN

PLATE XII

43. Bound for Count von Mansfelt, 1556

ALL SOULS COLLEGE

PLATE XIII

46. Bound by a Wotton binder, Paris, *c.* 1549
EXETER COLLEGE

PLATE XIV

47. Bound by a Wotton binder, Paris, *c.* 1549
EXETER COLLEGE

PLATE XV

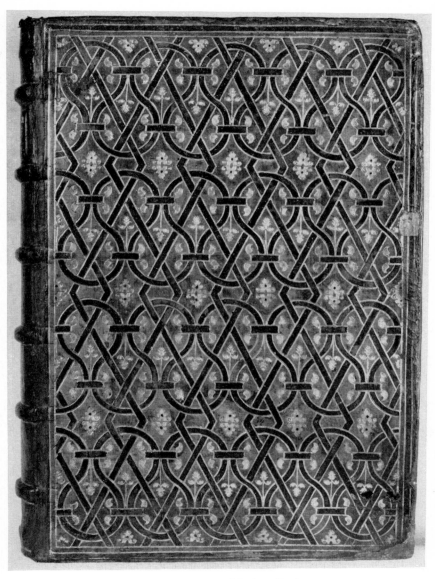

49. Bound by a Wotton binder, Paris, *c.* 1549
EXETER COLLEGE

PLATE XVI

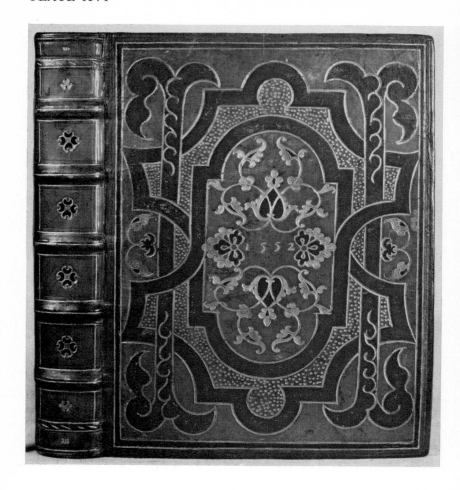

57. Bound for Thomas Wotton, Paris, *c.* 1552

PLATE XVII

65. Bound by the Medallion binder, England, *c.* 1545

ST. JOHN'S COLLEGE

PLATE XVIII

67. Bound for Henry VIII, England, *c.* 1545
TRINITY COLLEGE

PLATE XIX

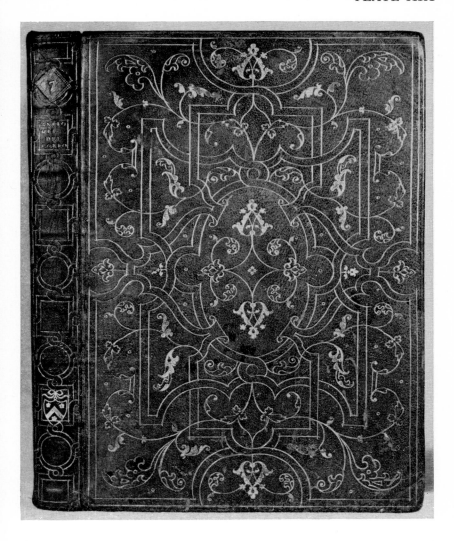

78. By one of Maioli's binders, Paris, *c.* 1550
ALL SOULS COLLEGE

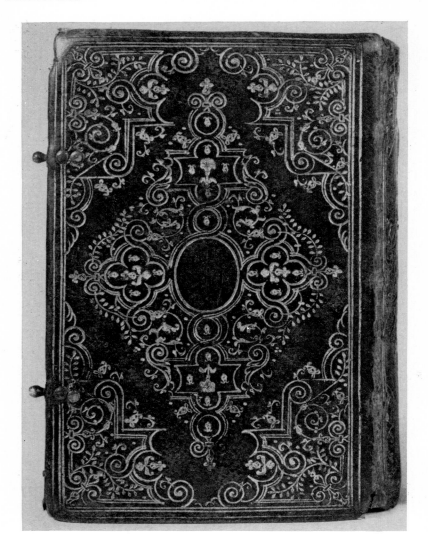

PLATE XX

87. Late fanfare style binding, Paris, *c.* 1600
SOMERVILLE COLLEGE

PLATE XXI

95. Duodo style binding, Paris, 1597?
KEBLE COLLEGE

PLATE XXII

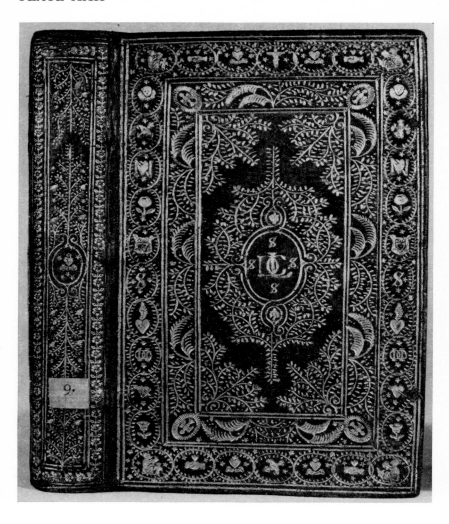

100. French binding with *S fermé*, *c.* 1600
BODLEIAN

PLATE XXIII

102. Binding possibly by Georges Drobet, Paris, 1587?
BODLEIAN

PLATE XXIV

108. Bound by the 'King's bookbinder', Geneva, 1572
CORPUS CHRISTI COLLEGE

PLATE XXV

110. Bound by the 'King's bookbinder', Geneva, *c.* 1580
ST. JOHN'S COLLEGE

PLATE XXVI

120. Bound for Matthew Parker, London, *c.* 1570
ALL SOULS COLLEGE

PLATE XXVII

126. Possibly bound by John de Planche, *c.* 1600
ST. JOHN'S COLLEGE

PLATE XXVIII

127. Benefactors' register, London, 1604
BODLEIAN

PLATE XXIX

129. Bound by Williamson, Eton, *c.* 1603
BODLEIAN

PLATE XXX

131. Bound for presentation to Sir Christopher Hatton, London, *c.* 1612
CHRIST CHURCH

PLATE XXXI

135. Bound for Francis Bacon, *c.* 1619
BODLEIAN

PLATE XXXII

137. Bound for George Villiers, *c.* 1625
JESUS COLLEGE

PLATE XXXIII

139. A London binding with the royal arms, c. 1627
ST. JOHN'S COLLEGE

PLATE XXXIV

140. Presentation binding for Smith's *Virginia*, *c*. 1624
QUEEN'S COLLEGE

PLATE XXXV

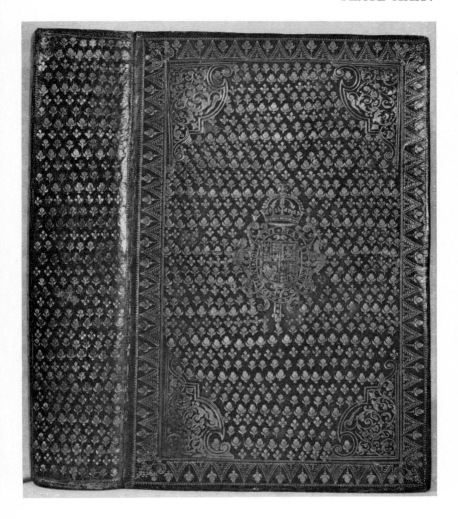

150. London binding with the royal arms, *c.* 1635

PLATE XXXVI

155. Possible Irish binding with the royal arms, *c.* 1640
WORCESTER COLLEGE

PLATE XXXVII

156. Cambridge binding, perhaps by John Houlden, *c.* 1643
BODLEIAN

PLATE XXXVIII

161. Cambridge binding by John Houlden, 1662
ST. JOHN'S COLLEGE

PLATE XXXIX

168. English embroidered medallion binding, c. 1640

BODLEIAN

PLATE XL

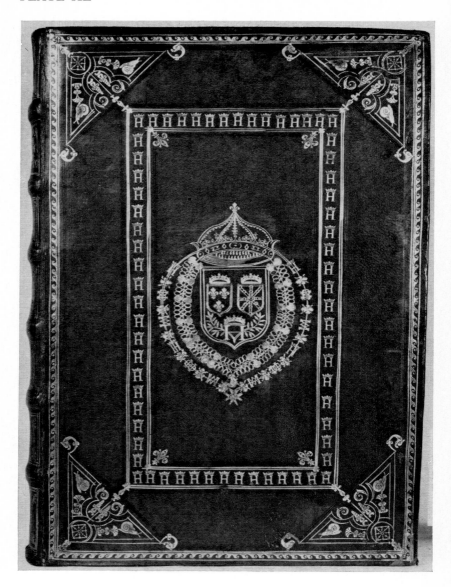

179. Italian binding for Henri IV, 1609
ALL SOULS COLLEGE

PLATE XLI

184. Italian transitional Baroque binding, *c.* 1600
BODLEIAN

PLATE XLII

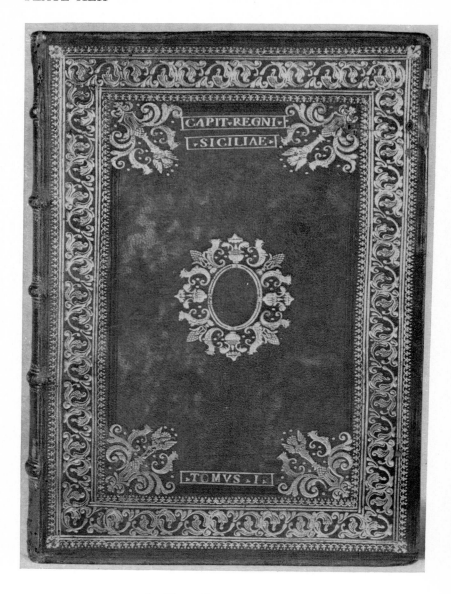

189. Neapolitan binding, 1614

PLATE XLIII

191. Inlaid *pointillé* binding, Paris, *c.* 1635
ST. JOHN'S COLLEGE

PLATE XLIV

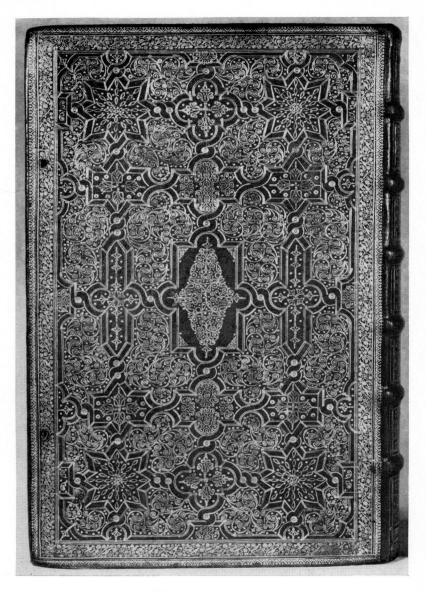

193. Dutch *pointillé* binding, Amsterdam? *c.* 1665
BODLEIAN

PLATE XLV

198. *Pointillé* binding with small head tool, Paris, 1647
BODLEIAN

PLATE XLVI

212. By the Royal heads binder, *c.* 1665
BODLEIAN

PLATE XLVII

215. Benefactors' register by Webb or Sedgley, Oxford, 1700
CORPUS CHRISTI COLLEGE

PLATE XLVIII

221. Bound by Samuel Mearne, London, 1669
LINCOLN COLLEGE

PLATE XLIX

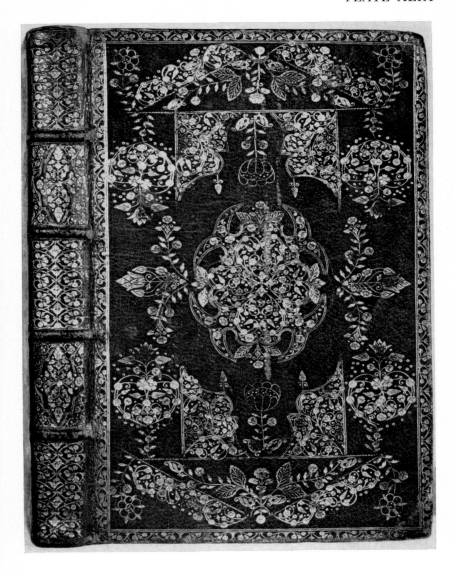

228. Bound by Roger Bartlett, Oxford, *c.* 1673

TRINITY COLLEGE

PLATE L

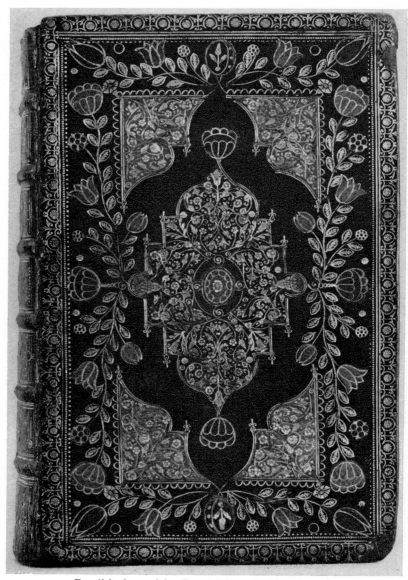

229. Possibly bound by Daniel Search, London, *c.* 1692
BODLEIAN

PLATE LI

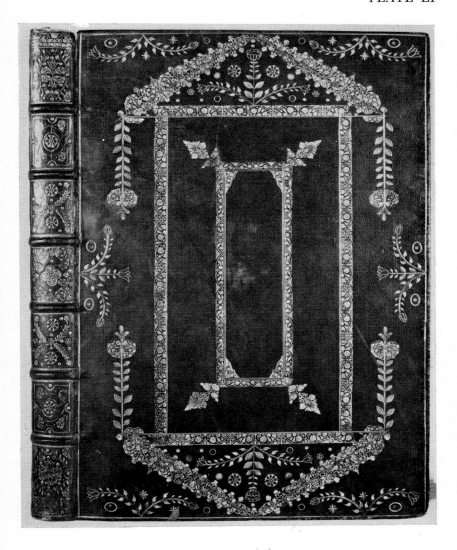

232. Possibly bound by Richard Sedgley, Oxford? *c.* 1690
EXETER COLLEGE

PLATE LII

237. Bound by the Queen's binder B, London, *c.* 1675
BODLEIAN